allegro-L

Winning Over Your Emotions

H. Norman Wright

HARVEST HOUSE PUBLISHERS
Eugene, Oregon 97402

Cover design by Terry Dugan Design, Minneapolis, Minnesota

WINNING OVER YOUR EMOTIONS
Copyright © 1998 by Harvest House Publishers
Eugene, Oregon 97402

Library of Congress Cataloging-in-Publication Data

Wright, H. Norman
    Winning over you emotions / H. Norman Wright.
        p.   cm.
    Includes bibliographical references.
    ISBN 1-56507-903-5
    1. Emotions—Religious aspects—Christianity.   I. Title.
BV4597.3.W75   1998   98-4087
248.8'6—dc21   CIP

Printed in the United States of America.

99 01 02 03 / BP / 10 9 8 7 6 5 4

Contents

The Answer to Worry

1

What Is Worry?

We are, perhaps, uniquely among the earth's
creatures the worrying animal. We worry away our
lives, fearing the future, discontent with the
present, unable to take in the idea of dying,
unable to sit still.

—LEWIS THOMAS

Worry: It knows no limits and has no boundaries. The poor worry about getting money and the wealthy worry about keeping it. It doesn't matter what age you are—worry could be your constant companion if you let it.

You've probably been in fog before. It's a misty moisture that puts a chill in the air and takes the curl out of your hair. Did you know, however, how much actual water is in fog? If there were a dense fog covering seven city blocks to a depth of 100 feet, the actual water content would be less than a glass of water! That's right—when it's condensed, all that fog, which slows traffic to a snail's pace and keeps you from seeing the building across the block, can fit into a drinking glass. The authors of *Helping Worriers* point out:

> Worry is like that. It clouds up reality. It chills us to the bone. It blocks the warmth and light of the sunshine. If we could see through the fog of worry and into the future, we would see our problems in their true light.[1]

Defining the Problem

How would you define worry? What sets it apart from anxiety or fear? When you experience anxiety, your body is responding. There's usually a muscle tightness and your heart is racing. Worry has been defined as the *thinking* part of anxiety, as a series of thoughts and images that are full of emotion—but all negative. These thoughts are rarely uncontrollable but they focus on something that has an uncertain outcome. The worrier is convinced beyond a shadow of a doubt that the outcome will be negative.

Worry comes from an Anglo-Saxon root meaning "to strangle" or "to choke." Worry is the uneasy, suffocating feeling we often experience in times of fear, trouble, or problems. When we worry, we look pessimistically into the future and think of the worst possible outcomes to the situations of our lives.

Remember that worry is basically focused on the future. Worry is the unnecessary fretting and stewing that keeps our minds stirred and our stomachs churning. Dr. W.C. Alvarez of the Mayo Clinic says, "Eighty percent of the stomach disorders that come to us are not organic, but functional. . . . Most of our ills are caused by worry and fear."[2] Intense worry is about as useful to our thinking as lighted matches in a dynamite factory.

We raise golden retrievers. We don't let them have bones to chew on because they're not good for them. But have you ever seen a dog with a bone? We have a phrase for the way a dog becomes addicted to that bone: He "worries" it. He just gnaws and gnaws on it day and night. He won't let go and may growl at you if you try to take it away from him. He's looking for meat but usually finds gristle, bone, and marrow. The dog will bury his bone, then dig it up and gnaw on it again even though it's covered with dirt and leaves. He'll bury it and repeat the process again and again. Worriers are the same: They bite and chew on their worry, bury it, dig it up, bury it, and dig it up again.

The War Within Us

Worry is like a war that is quietly raging inside us. John Haggai describes the conflict this way:

> Worry divides the feelings; therefore the emotions lack stability. Worry divides the understanding; therefore convictions are shallow and changeable. Worry divides the faculty of perception; therefore observations are faulty and even false. Worry divides the faculty of judging; therefore attitudes and decisions are often unjust. These decisions lead to damage and grief. Worry divides the determinative faculty; therefore plans and purposes, if not "scrapped" altogether, are not filled with persistence.[3]

Worry is thinking turned into poisoned thoughts. Worry has been described as a small trickle of fear that meanders through the mind until it cuts a channel into which all other thoughts are drained.

With worry there is a dread of something just over the horizon. When you worry you are preoccupied with something about yourself. And often you keep the worries to yourself. This tendency keeps you on edge. You're not fully relaxed.

In fact, worriers don't handle stress or upset as well as others. They're overly troubled by it. Worry has been called the fuel system for stress. When you worry, you add to your upset by coming up with several worst-case scenarios to your concern, but you're unable to know for sure which one is going to happen.

A worrier has a calling in life: He wants to examine what can go wrong. He is like the driver on the freeway who comes upon a grisly accident. It's horrible, but he has to look. Why? Because of fear and curiosity. A worrier is someone who puts his hand into a hole or box and feels around to see if anything is in there that could bite him. He can't leave it alone.

Worry is like a magnet that draws the worrier. Perhaps we're all interested in what can go wrong in our life. We're fascinated by the possibilities. And when a possibility is discovered, we latch onto it with all of our "what ifs."[4]

Worry is a special kind of fear. To create it, we elongate fear with two things—anticipation and memory. We then infuse it with our imagination and feed it with emotion. And then we have our creation.[5]

You've heard of the word "catastrophe," and that's what a worrier envisions. In his mind he creates the worst of all possible outcomes.[6]

Did you know that worry affects your sleep? Some people tend to sleep on and on as though it's a rest from the drain of worry, but for most people worry is likely to create insomnia. The thoughts that race and tumble through your worrisome mind interfere with your ability to relax and fall asleep.

There are other things that happen to your body when you worry. You may not be aware of them, but they are there. It takes an electroencephalogram (EEG) to show you. This test shows the brainwave differences which occur when people worry. A worrier actually has fewer of the brainwaves that help a person to relax. In fact, cortical activity actually increases.

When you worry excessively, your brain is heavily impacted. The more you worry about something (and I mean hours a day, week after week) it's as though one of your brain's "switching stations" gets stuck. Remember when you have a cramp in a leg muscle and it stays and stays regardless of what you do? Well, it's as though you have a brain cramp and it won't let go of your worry. The more you worry the more you cut a groove in your brain, and the more worry finds a home in which to reside. That's why other people's suggestions of "Don't worry" or "Just relax" won't work.

What happens if you experience a major upset in your life? Then there is even more of a biological process that occurs. Your body goes into action, sending out various hormones and other substances in its response to the trauma. This actually makes the worry "burn" itself into the brain. It really becomes attached, and your brain's physical state changes. It can actually alter your brain's chemistry.[7]

Worry and Anxiety

If fear and worry are first cousins, worry and anxiety have an even closer relationship. Worry and anxiety both refer to the inner turmoil we experience in fearful, stressful situations. The Greeks described anxiety as opposing forces at work to tear a man apart.

We all worry; that's a given. But many Christians worry excessively and thus end up suffering. Their worry is more than an annoyance; it actually hinders their lives.

There is a place in our lives for legitimate fear and concern, and at times a degree of anxiety when these are related to realistic situations. Not all anxiety is bad; it sometimes has a plus side. As Dr. Quentin Hyder suggests in *The Christian's Handbook of Psychiatry:*

> A little [anxiety] in normal amounts can enhance performance. Athletes would be unable to perform successfully without it. Businessmen do better in their competitive world than they could do without its stimulus. It definitely strengthens concentration and spurs imagination, thereby producing more creative ideas. It stimulates interest and develops ambition. It protects from danger.[8]

In its positive sense, anxiety is a God-given instinct that alerts us to fearful situations and prepares us to respond appropriately to them. But worry often takes a concern and makes it toxic. The *legitimate* responses form a built-in alarm system that works when needed, but worry is like a car alarm system that won't turn off and can drive the frustrated owner up a wall!

There are many diseases in our world today, but worry is an old one—a disease of the imagination. It's like a virus that slowly and subtly overtakes and dominates your life. It's like an invading army which creeps ashore at night and eventually controls the country. When that happens, your ability to live life the way you want to is diminished. A Swedish proverb says, "Worry gives a small thing a big shadow."

Again, the negative aspects of worry and anxiety must be differentiated from positive concern in troublesome situations. Pastor Earl Lee illustrates the difference:

> Worry is like racing an automobile engine while it is in neutral. The gas and noise and smog do not get us anywhere. But legitimate concern . . . is putting the car into low gear on your way to moving ahead. You tell yourself that you are going to use the power God has given you to do something about the situation which could cause you to fret.[9]

Worry immobilizes you and does not lead to action, while legitimate concern moves you to overcome the problem.

Many Scripture verses describe the effects of fear, worry, and anxiety. And many other verses reveal that a worry-free life reaps many positive rewards. Notice the contrast in the verses below:

> I heard, and my [whole inner self] trembled; my lips quivered at the sound. Rottenness enters into my bones and under me [down to my feet]; I tremble (Habakkuk 3:16 AMP).

> Anxiety in a man's heart weighs it down (Proverbs 12:25 AMP).

> A tranquil mind gives life to the flesh (Proverbs 14:30 RSVB).

> All the days of the desponding and afflicted are made evil [by anxious thoughts and forebodings], but he who has a glad heart has a continual feast [regardless of circumstances] (Proverbs 15:15 AMP).

A happy heart is a good medicine and a cheerful mind works healing, but a broken spirit dries the bones (Proverbs 17:22 AMP).

A glad heart makes a cheerful countenance, but by sorrow of heart the spirit is broken (Proverbs 15:13 AMP).

2

What Are You Worried About?

What do people worry about? It would be safe to say *everything*. Dr. Samuel Kraines and Eloise Thetford suggest three categories into which most worries fall:

1. Disturbing situations for which one must find a *solution*—for example, how to obtain money for food, lodging, or medical expenses.

2. Disturbing situations over which one has *no control*—for example, a mother dying of cancer, a usually prompt daughter who is five hours late, or a son in active combat.

3. Unimportant, insignificant, *minor problems of everyday life which warrant little attention,* let alone "worry." People "worry" about minor details of everyday life, concocting horrible possibilities and then "stewing" about them. The housewife "worries" that she cannot clean the house as she once did, does not iron the clothes well, and cannot prepare proper meals. The man "worries" that he is doing poorly at work, that he will be "fired," and that he "cannot pay his bills." The list goes on and on. The worry is not only a feeling tone of fearfulness but an overriding sense of futility, hopelessness, and dreaded possibilities.[10]

Worrying intensely about the possibility of some event happening not only fails to prevent it from occurring but can actually help to bring it about. A young seminary student is waiting to preach his first sermon. He sits thinking about what he is going to say. He begins to worry about forgetting words, stumbling over certain phrases, and not presenting himself in a confident manner. As he continues to worry, he actually sees himself making these mistakes. And then when he gets up to preach, he makes the very mistakes he worried about!

If you were to tell him he shouldn't worry about his preaching, he would reply, "I was justified in worrying. After all, those problems that I worried about were real problems. They happened, didn't they? I should have been worried." What he doesn't realize is that by his own worry he actually helped them occur. He was responsible for his own failure. He spent more time seeing himself fail than he did visualizing himself succeeding or overcoming his fears.

Doing What You Think

The principle here is that if you spend time seeing yourself as a failure, you will more than likely reproduce that example in your performance. You actually condition yourself for negative performances because of your negative thinking. The classic example is the person who worries about getting an ulcer and in a few months is rewarded for his efforts with an ulcer. People who continually worry about having an accident on the freeway are very accident-prone. They are more likely to have accidents than other people because they constantly visualize the event.

However, if you spend the same amount of time and energy planning how to overcome your anticipated mistakes and envisioning your success as you do visualizing your failure, your performance will be far better. Proverbs 23:7 tells us that the way we think in our hearts determines what we do.

The final results of fear, worry, and anxiety are negative, self-defeating, and incapacitating. What do we accomplish by worrying? Are there any positive results? Make a list of the things you worry about, then describe specifically what the worry has accomplished or will accomplish. Does it solve the problem or does it create more problems?

When you worry about a problem, real or imaginary, it usually impedes you from being able to do something effective about the problem. Worry, in other words, is a big problem in itself.

Do you enjoy worrying? Worry seems to have a certain attraction in itself. Pain seems to grab our attention more readily than pleasure. Perhaps worrying is a bit like watching a scary horror movie: It's kind of exciting as well as entertaining. Or perhaps when you worry, you're getting some kind of stimulation. Your mind is engaged, locked in on a target like radar looking for a heat-seeking missile.

A Protective Device?

Have you ever considered worry as a protective device? For some people it is. It's as though the worry portion of the brain has a spasm. It just can't seem to let go of the perceived problem and see the other side. Whatever the good news is, it's rejected.

Those who are depressed often turn to worry. If you have an obsessive-compulsive condition, worry can come as the waves of an ocean. You can't seem to stop it. If you were traumatized, worry is your constant companion.

Part of the solution is to first learn as much as you can about worry and anxiety. Don't run from it, and don't believe that it cannot be overcome. It can.

Sometimes it helps to *take action* rather than give in to the worry. If what you are worrying about needs some action, then take some action. Immobility feeds worry just as it feeds depression.

Perhaps you've seen films of the inside of a cockpit of a fighter plane. Most of our planes rely upon missiles for their weaponry. In front of the pilot is a screen which shows the enemy plane. The pilot guides the flight of his plane in order to line it up for the missile. When he does this the screen lights up with a "missile lock" message. The missile is locked onto that enemy plane until it's destroyed.

In the same way this worry cluster seems to lock on to the problem and won't let go. Then it sends an alarm signal to the front part of the brain, which analyzes the worry. Now the front portion sends a signal back to the cluster, which says, "I'm worrying now." The cluster is alarmed even more and sends signals back to the front, and thus it goes on and on. It's like a circuit that can't be broken. It's as though worry has taken control of the brain and shuts out the rest of life around you.

The Role of Physiology

Many individuals choose or learn to worry, but only recently the role of physiology has been discovered to also be involved in worry. An article in the November 29, 1996, issue of the *New York Times* described a study by Dr. Dennis Murphy at the U.S. National Institute of Mental Health and Klause-Peter Lesch of the University of Wurzburg in Germany. The study indicated a gene which regulates one of the chemicals in our body called serotonin. You may be surprised by this next piece of information. On the other hand, you may be like some who would say, "I knew it all along!"

If a person has this gene, he may have an inclination to worry. Some people actually look for an issue to worry about, since the only time they feel complete is when they do so.

When we are born we come into an inheritance. In fact it's been given to us prior to birth during the development process. It's as though we sit through the reading of a will and discover what our inheritance is going to be. Some of what we inherit makes life fuller and easier, while some has the opposite effect.

You may have inherited the tendency to be shy. Or you may have a nervous system and structure that are high-strung. Some people have a trigger mechanism for worry that is a hair trigger; the slightest touch sets it off. Some develop this over years of practice, but others are born this way.

Technicians wire up computers, components, and other electronic instruments in certain ways, and we are all wired in unique ways as well. When we enter this life we have a certain set of personality traits—or wiring, as it were. Some of us are wired to be extroverts and some of us to be introverts. Some of us are methodical and structured while others can become lost between the front door and the car.

Dr. Edward Hallowell described our condition very well when he said:

> Worries seem to inherit a neurological vulnerability that life events can then trigger . . . while some people are born confident, others are born insecure, while some people are born calm, others are born wired, while some people are born plunging forward, others are born holding back. You may be born with a specific characteristic or you may be born with a vulnerability to develop it later on, in the face of the stresses life usually presents.[11]

However, before any of us say, "That's it. That's the reason I worry: I can't help it. I'm genetically predisposed and predetermined to do so. Nothing I do will ever help, so why try?" consider these factors:

1. None of us knows for sure if that is the reason at this point in time.

2. This predisposition is also modified by our personality and life experiences. What we experience and learn in life can have an effect on how strongly a gene may be expressed, and (here is the big factor) *the expression of*

such a gene can be changed by experience and training.
Regardless of the reason we worry, we *can* learn to control
its effect upon our lives. As Christians, we have the greatest opportunity to do so because of the resources of our
faith.[12]

Anxiety

Anxiety was mentioned earlier, but let's look at it further
to see how it differs from worry. Anxiety is a painful or appre-
hensive uneasiness of mind tied into some impending event.
It's a response full of fear that impacts the body with responses
that include sweating, muscles tensing, rapid pulse rate, and
fast breathing. There is also a sense of doubt about both the
reality of the threat and one's ability to handle it.

We all experience anxiety, but when it disrupts our
lifestyle we call it an *anxiety disorder*. Most anxiety is
self-induced, but how does it develop? In fact, it tends to run
in families. There appears to be some type of genetic bent
toward this tendency, just like worry. Your environment also
plays a role. This could include a family member who provided
a role model of being a worrier, the expectation for you to be
perfect, some form of abandonment as a child, and so on.

Anxiety can be influenced by biochemistry as well. Some
of the personality traits that we develop can also contribute to
an anxiety disorder, including the tendency to have huge
expectations as well as to need the approval of everyone.
When your mind dwells on these things it affects your biochemistry, which can then make you more prone to being
anxious.

We call this the *adrenaline response*. A signal is sent to
your brain, and an alarm system is activated. Your body then
secretes a hormone called adrenaline. (That's just the beginning of the process.) Your nervous system has been warned
that something is wrong, that some danger may be present or
possible. Then cortisol is secreted. These stimulants begin to
flow through your body.

This biochemical response is *not* a malfunction of the central nervous system; it is a completely normal response. In fact it is part of your survival mechanism. If someone wearing a ski mask were to burst into your home, your body would immediately respond by registering trouble. Then adrenaline and cortisol would start racing through your body. God created you with a central nervous system which is sensitive when it receives these stimulants. It reacts with the "flight-or-fight" response.

You are now ready to either defend yourself or run away as fast as you can. Your system is prepared for survival. This is an appropriate response from a healthy, functioning system trying to protect itself. You're normal, and your body has gone into action. It's on call to protect you.

Have you ever experienced getting worked up in your mind? You create a scenario in your thought life that is as real as life itself. The same bodily response happens, as though you're confronted with the intruder in the ski mask.

Your heart begins to pump faster as it transports oxygen to the muscles in your legs and arms. Your stomach contracts as blood moves swiftly away from it. If you experience a chronically upset stomach, nausea, or cramping, you may think, "What if I have stomach cancer?" Blood rushes into your arms and legs and out of your hands and feet. Your fingers and toes become cold. They tingle. So now you think, "What if I have multiple sclerosis?" Your heart pounds so hard that you think, "Oh no! What if I'm having a heart attack?" The blood rushes out of your head, which causes you to be dizzy, so you think, "What if I have a brain tumor?" There is nothing to be done with your overstimulated system, so you turn it on itself. This is just one step away from panic.[13]

Have you ever felt so anxious that you've been bewildered or even disoriented? You may have felt, "Oh no! I'm losing my mind! I'm going crazy!" You probably want to get rid of this bewildered feeling because you think it's bad. But actually it is a healthy response that helps you cope with the situation. If you struggle with excessive anxiety or any kind of phobias you could experience these responses. *This is your mind's way of taking a break or minivacation from your emotional overload.*

In a crisis or a trauma a person's normal system shuts down and a mild state of shock goes into action. The system needs to shut down because there is too much coming at the person for him to handle everything. His senses can't handle it all.

When you experience excessive anxiety the same thing happens. This is an adrenaline response. It won't hurt you and it will go away in a few hours. Instead of focusing on your fear, which will produce more adrenaline, tell yourself, "I'm all right; this is normal. God created my body to respond this way. This is protecting me from too much happening at once."

You may ask, "What can I do if I've triggered the chemical response?" You can still reverse it. Take a pen and paper and write. Purposely do something you enjoy. Do something totally different.

Personality and Anxiety

Now let's consider some of the personality traits that can contribute to anxiety in our lives.

Perfectionism is one culprit. It's an impossibility. It's an exercise in frustration. I've never yet met a successful perfectionist. You can use the same energy to develop high standards and pursue excellence. With perfectionism you're never satisfied, but with excellence you can be. When you know you've done your best, you can gain a sense of enjoyment. Take your energy and work toward becoming comfortable with the fact that things aren't perfect and never will be.

Another culprit is how you interpret the feelings you have inside. Perhaps you decide to go river rafting. As you approach the rapids and see the water churning and frothing, your heart pounds, your hands are sweaty, and you have difficulty breathing. What do you say to yourself? You could say,

"I'm terrified. I'm going to drown. They'll never find my body." You're filled with fear. You feel panicky.

Or you could say, "This is wild. It's so exciting. What a trip! It's okay for my heart to pound and my palms to be this sweaty." By saying this, you'll feel *excitement* rather than fear.[14]

There is another simple way to tackle the "what ifs" of worry and anxiety: Just take every anxious or worrisome "what if" and turn it around to make it positive. Here are some examples:

· "What if I never get over my worry?" to "What if I do overcome my worry?"

"What if I forget what I'm supposed to say?" to "What if I remember everything I want to say?"

"What if I mess up and lose my job?" to "What if I do all right and keep my job?"

"What if I never get off this medication?" to "What if I get off my medication?"

"What if those new people don't like me?" to "What if the new people really like me?"

"What if I fail that test?" to "What if I pass the test and do very well?"

The negative way of thinking creates more worry and anxiety; the positive way creates anticipation, excitement, and hope.

The Principle of Replacement

Another way of handling your anxiety is to *counter* your negative thoughts. It's the principle of replacement. Yes, it will take time, effort, and repetition, but it will be effective.

The following are some examples of typical negative thoughts and some suggestions on how you can challenge them and shift them to positive thoughts:

Negative: When will I ever get over these panic feelings? I feel so afraid sometimes and this drains my energy.

Positive: I'm working on overcoming these panic attacks. Will these hurt me? No. I'll just let these feelings come when they want to, and eventually they'll go away.

Negative: I feel as if my anxious feelings are controlling my life. I hate this situation. I feel stuck.

Positive: So . . . it's just anxiety. It's no big deal. Anxiety is a part of life. I'm doing better. I'm learning to control it. I'm better this week than I was last week. It will take time but I will conquer it with the Lord's help.

Negative: I don't want to go anywhere today. What if I get sick?

Positive: It's okay to feel these feelings. I haven't gone anywhere for a long time. I'm not going to be sick. I'm okay. I'll be just fine. I'll focus on how I can enjoy this outing. It's never as bad as I anticipate it to be.

Negative: Sometimes I feel like I'm never going to get control of my anxiety and worry. It's like a deeply ingrained habit!

Positive: Look how I've grown already. Imagine where I'll be in six weeks or months! I'm doing well. I can thank God for the changes that have occurred in my life.

Negative: Why is that person so mad at me? Did I do something? Is it something I said?

Positive: I'm taking this much too seriously. How do I know he's mad at me? I don't. If he's mad, it's his concern, not mine. It's up to him to tell me if it's me.

Negative: What if I try the new job and I don't like it or don't do well? I'd feel so upset.

Positive: Trying is an accomplishment! If it doesn't work out, at least I took the chance. That in itself is a new and positive step.

Negative: These anxious feelings make me feel like I'm losing my mind. They're so unpleasant.

Positive: I know what these feelings cause. I know I'm emotional and I didn't eat right. It isn't worth getting anxious about. I'll feel better in the future.[15]

Anxiety may stem from unconscious feelings, but worry is a conscious act of choosing an ineffective method of coping with life. Oswald Chambers has said that all our fret and worry is caused by calculating without God. When we choose to worry it implies an absence of trust in God. And since Scripture specifically instructs us *not* to worry, this lack of trust in the Lord is certainly sin. But keep in mind that when a person is genetically wired toward the tendency to worry, this is not a sin. It is simply a result of the distorting of the human race, which is a result of Adam's sin. Not choosing to learn how to lessen or overcome the worry is the problem in this case.

The OCD Syndrome

One of the most intense expréssions of worry is OCD—Obsessive Compulsive Disorder. Worry seems to rule the mind like a tyrant! Certain thoughts come into your mind that you can't evict. The person affected with OCD has a variety of intense, unwanted thoughts that he or she is obsessed with. Sometimes he feels compelled to do certain rituals which are supposed to keep specific consequences from occurring. It could be turning off the faucet a certain way five times, closing all the doors, lining up the papers on a desk to match perfectly, having all the cans spaced perfectly in the cupboards, and so forth.

Between 1 and 3 percent of our population experience this syndrome. In a way OCD is an intensification of the fears and worries that most people experience, but with OCD these fears dominate their life. One of the best descriptions of this disorder was written by Judith Rapoport in her book *The Boy Who Couldn't Stop Washing*. There are various treatments available today for this disorder. For an in-depth look at this problem see *When Once Is Not Enough,* by Gail Steketee, Ph.D., and Kevin White, M.D. (New Harbinger Publications).

One of the ways to deal with intense worries or anxiety is to face your fears head-on. The more we run from our fears, the larger they grow. The best way to deal with them is to face them directly. In baseball there is a guideline that infielders follow: "Play the ground ball, don't let the ground ball play you." What this means is that when a ground ball is hit to you, in order to field it cleanly there's one step to follow: Instead of backing up and trying to predict the bounces as the ball comes to you, do just the opposite. (You don't want to be at the mercy of the unpredictable bounces it makes. This is called letting the ball play you.) *Charge the ball,* and in doing this you'll act rather than think too much. You'll grab the ball before you have a chance to think yourself into making an error.

Other Solutions

If you really are afraid of something, try exposing yourself to it a little bit at a time until you're comfortable with it. Years ago a woman came to see me who was deathly afraid of earthquakes. Now that's one of the four seasons we have in Southern California—earthquakes. They're kind of hard to avoid. She had been through the Sylmar earthquake in the early seventies and was traumatized by it. She worried every day that she would go through another one. She was so fearful that for the past ten years she had avoided reading newspapers and listening to or watching any news programs in order to avoid hearing about any earthquakes. This did nothing but intensify her fears.

Finally she realized that this was no way to live, so she came for help. We worked together for several months. Each week we talked a bit more about earthquakes. She learned to face them rather than run from them. She graduated from counseling after she went to the library, checked out a book on earthquakes, and read it. She realized that she will experience more of these in her lifetime and will have to deal with each one when it comes. But for now, she didn't need to worry about the next one. She faced her fears slowly and consistently, and gradually she broke the hold they had on her.

Sometimes worry or anxiety is so intense that for a while medication is a helpful solution. It can help the anxious or worried brain put on the brakes. Medication is not a cure-all but is simply one of several forms of treatment. It should be used only when indicated, and only a physician should be the one to prescribe it (sometimes in conjunction with a counselor or a therapist). Medication should never be prescribed by oneself.

What are some of the medications? You've probably heard of Valium, which is a benzodiazepine. There are many similar medications, and they simply put a damper on the excessive activity going on in the brain. Remember, medication is a legitimate help but it's not a permanent cure. And you may have to contend with some side effects. But again, the decision to prescribe a medication is not yours but a physician's.

3

$\mathscr{B}$iblical Answers to Worry

Does worry have any place in the life of the Christian? Is it a sin to worry or to feel anxiety?

A person who experiences extreme states of anxiety may not be able to control them. He may feel he is at the mercy of his feelings because he cannot pin down exactly why he is so anxious. This person may have deep, hidden feelings or hurts that have lingered for years in the subconscious. In such a case, perhaps he needs to face the problem, discover the roots of his feelings, and replace them with the healing power and resources offered through Jesus Christ and Scripture.

But freedom from worry *is possible*. The answer lies in tapping the resources of Scripture. Read each passage cited below before reading the paragraphs that follow it.

Worry doesn't work, so don't do it (Matthew 6:25-34). From this passage we can discover several principles to help us overcome anxiety and worry. First, note that Jesus did *not* say, "Stop worrying when everything is going all right for you." His command is not a suggestion. He simply and directly said to stop worrying about your life. In a way, Jesus was saying we should learn to accept situations that cannot be altered at the present time. That doesn't mean we're to sit back and make no attempt to improve conditions around us. But we must face tough situations without worry and learn to live with them while we work toward improvement.

Second, Jesus said you cannot add any length of time to your life span by worrying. Not only is this true, but the reverse is also true: The physical effects of worry can actually shorten your life span.

Third, the object of our worry may be a part of the difficulty. It could be that our sense of values is distorted and that what we worry about should not be the center of our attention. The material items that seem so important to us should be secondary to spiritual values.

Fourth, Christ also tells us to live a day at a time. You may be able to change some of the results of past behavior, but you cannot change the past, so don't worry about it. You cannot predict or completely prepare for the future, so don't inhibit its potential by worrying about it. Focus your energies on the opportunities of today!

Most of the future events that people worry about don't happen anyway. Furthermore, the worrisome anticipation of certain inevitable events is usually more distressing than the actual experience itself. Anticipation is the magnifying glass of our emotions. And even if an event is as serious as we may anticipate, the Christian can look forward to God's supply of strength and stability at all times.

Focus on the solution, not the problem (Matthew 14:22-33). In this passage, we find the disciples in a boat as Jesus walked toward them on the water. When Peter began to walk toward Jesus on the water, he was fine until his attention was drawn away from Jesus to the storm. Then he became afraid and started to sink.

If Peter had kept his attention upon Christ (the source of his strength and the solution to his problem), he would have been all right. But when he focused upon the wind and the waves (the problem and the negative aspect of his circumstances), he became overwhelmed by the problem, even though he could have made it safely to Jesus.

Worry is like that. We focus so hard on the problem that we take our eyes off the solution and thus create more difficulties for ourselves. We can be sustained in the midst of any difficulty by focusing our attention on the Lord and relying upon Him.

> Blessed is the man who trusts in the LORD, whose confidence is in him. He will be like a tree planted by the water that sends out its roots by the stream. It does not fear when heat comes; its leaves are always green. It has no worries in a year of drought and never fails to bear fruit. The heart is deceitful above all things and beyond cure. Who can understand it? "I the LORD search the heart and examine the mind, to reward a man according to his conduct, according to what his deeds deserve" (Jeremiah 17:7-10).

Make a Choice

You and I live in an unstable world. As I'm writing this, the stock market has just dropped several hundred points. This has not only created worry but also fear, anxiety, and panic in some people. But when we trust in the Lord (and not the stock market) we receive the blessing of stability in a fragmented world. We have the ability to be free from worry in a world where there is much to be anxious and fearful about.

Did you ever see the passage in Luke 21:14,15?

> Make up your mind not to worry beforehand how you will defend yourselves. For I will give you words and wisdom that none of your adversaries will be able to resist or contradict.

At the beginning of the verse is a phrase that is a command but also implies that we have the capability of doing it. "Make up your mind" means we have a choice as to whether *we choose* to worry or *choose not* to worry. "Make up your mind" comes from a Greek word which means "to premeditate." You've probably heard this word used in criminal trials.

If someone is accused of a premeditated crime, it means he thought it through beforehand. Choosing not to worry will take more effort and energy for some people than others, but change is possible.

Give God your worry in advance (1 Peter 5:7). Peter must have learned from his experience of walking on the water because he later wrote: "Cast all your anxiety on him [God] because he cares for you." "Cast" means "to give up" or "to unload." The tense of the verb here refers to a direct, once-and-for-all committal to God of all anxiety or worry. We are to unload on God our tendency to worry, so that when problems arise, we will not worry about them. We can cast our worry on God with confidence because He cares for us. He is not out to break us down, but to strengthen us and to help us stand firm. He knows our limits, and "a bruised reed he will not break, and a dimly burning wick he will not quench" (Isaiah 42:3 RSVB).

Center your thought on God, not on worry (Isaiah 26:3). Isaiah rejoiced to the Lord, "You will guard him and keep him in perfect and constant peace whose mind [both its inclination and its character] is stayed on You" (AMP). Whatever you choose to think about will either produce or dismiss feelings of anxiety and worry. Those people who suffer from worry are choosing to center their minds on negative thoughts and to anticipate the worst. But if your mind or imagination is centered on God—what He has done and will do for you—and the promises of Scripture, peace of mind is inevitable. But *you must choose* to center your thoughts in this way. God has made the provision, but *you must take the action.* Freedom from worry and anxiety is available, but you must lay hold of it.

Replace fretting with trust (Psalm 37:1-40). Psalm 37:1 begins, "Do not fret," and those words are repeated later in the psalm. The dictionary defines "fret" as "to eat away, gnaw, gall, vex, worry, agitate, wear away."

Whenever I hear this word, I'm reminded of the scene I see each year when I hike along the Snake River in the Grand

Teton National Park in Wyoming. Colonies of beavers live along the riverbanks, and often I see trees at various stages of being gnawed to the ground by them. Some trees have slight rings around their trunks where the beavers have just started to chew on them. Other trees have several inches of bark eaten away, and some have already fallen to the ground because the beavers have gnawed through the trunks. Worry has the same effect on us: It will gradually eat away at us until it destroys us.

The Positive Substitutes

In addition to telling us not to fret, Psalm 37 gives us positive substitutes for worry. First, it says, "Trust (lean on, rely on, and be confident) in the Lord" (verse 3 AMP). Trust is a matter of not attempting to live an independent life or to cope with difficulties alone. It means going to a greater source for strength.

Second, verse 4 says, "Delight yourself also in the Lord" (AMP). To delight means to rejoice in God and what He has done for us, to let God supply the joy for our life.

Third, verse 5 says, "Commit your way to the Lord" (AMP). Commitment is a definite act of the will, and it involves releasing our worries and anxieties to the Lord.

And fourth, we are to "rest in the Lord; wait for Him" (verse 7 AMP). This means to submit in silence to what He ordains, and to be ready and expectant for what He is going to do in our life.

Stop worrying and start praying (Philippians 4:6-9; Psalm 34:1-4). The passage in Philippians can be divided into three basic stages. We are given a *premise:* Stop worrying. We are given a *practice:* Start praying. And we are given a *promise:* Peace. The promise is there and available, but we must follow the first two steps in order for the third to occur. We must stop worrying and start praying if we are to begin receiving God's peace.

The results of prayer as a substitute for worry can be vividly seen in a crisis in David's life that prompted him to write Psalm 34. (See 1 Samuel 21:10–22:2.) David had escaped death at the hands of the Philistines by pretending to be insane. He then fled to the cave of Adullam along with 400 men who were described as distressed, discontented, and in debt. In the midst of all this, David wrote a psalm of praise that begins, "I will bless the Lord at all times; his praise shall continually be in my mouth" (Psalm 34:1 RSVB). He did not say he would praise the Lord *sometimes, but at all times*, even when his enemies were after him.

How could David bless the Lord in the midst of his life-threatening experience? Because he stopped worrying and started praying: "I sought the Lord, and he answered me, and delivered me from all my fears" (verse 4 RSVB). David didn't turn around and take his cares back after he had deposited them with the Lord. He gave them up. Too many people give their burdens to God with a rubber band attached. As soon as they stop praying, the problems bounce back. They pray, "Give us this day our daily bread," and as soon as they are through praying, they begin to worry where their next meal is going to come from.

Another factor to notice is that God did not take David away from his problem in order to deliver him from his fears. David was still hiding in the cave with 400 disgruntled men when he wrote the psalm. God does not always take us out of problematic situations, but He gives us the peace we seek as we proceed prayerfully through each experience. It happened to David, and it happens today to those who pray, unload their cares on God, and leave them there.

> Do not fear, for I am with you; do not be dismayed, for I am your God. I will strengthen you and help you; I will uphold you with my righteous right hand (Isaiah 41:10).

This verse tells us not to fear, but then tells us why: "For I am with you." There is no better reason to stop being fearful or worried than the one given here: God is with you. In the phrase "Do not be dismayed," the word for "dismayed" means "to gaze," to look around in an anxious way. This word is used to describe a person who is looking around in amazement or bewilderment. It's the idea of being immobilized or paralyzed. You can't make up your mind which way to turn.

But once again there is a solution: God says, "I am your God." He is with us not eight hours a day, not 12 or 16, but 24 hours each day. When He says, "I will strengthen you," the words mean "to be alert" or "to be fortified with courage." When He says, "I will help you," the word "help" means "to summon." Imagine yourself surrounded by the loving arms of God. In fact each time you worry, make the statement "I am surrounded by the loving arms of God," and see whether your worry wants to stick around. The last words, "I will uphold you," mean to sustain. In music, when the conductor tells the singers to "sustain that note" they keep singing it on and on until they've exhausted their air supply. But there is no exhaustion on God's part in sustaining us.[16]

Breaking the Worry Pattern

Again and again the Scriptures give us the answer for fears and worries. You may be aware of the resources of Scripture on the subject, but do you know *how* to break the worry pattern in your own life? I'm talking about practical strategies by which you can apply the guidelines of Scripture to your specific worries. Let me share with you a few tips that others have used successfully over the years.

Make a value judgment on worry. Let me illustrate the first suggestion by taking you into my counseling office. I was working with a man who had a roaring tendency to worry. We had talked through the reasons for his worry, and he had tried some of my suggestions for conquering his problem. But it seemed to me that he was resistant to giving up his worry. This isn't unusual; many people have worried for so long that they have grown comfortable with their negative patterns of thinking. It's actually all they know. They're successful with it and are unsure they will be successful with the new style of thinking.

So one day I gave him an assignment that really caught him off guard: "It appears that worry is an integral part of your life and that you are determined to keep this tendency. But you only worry periodically throughout the day, with no real plan for worrying. So let's set up a definite worry time for you each day instead of spreading it out.

"Tomorrow when you begin to worry about something, instead of worrying at that moment, write down what you're worried about on an index card and keep the card in your pocket. Each time a worry pops up, write it on the card, but don't worry about it yet. Then about 4:00 P.M., go into a room where you can be alone. Sit down, take out the card, and worry about those items as intensely as you can for 30 minutes. Start the next day with a new blank card and do the same thing. What do you think about that idea?"

He stared at me in silence for several moments. "That's got to be one of the dumbest suggestions I've ever heard," he answered finally. "I can't believe I'm paying you to hear advice like that."

I smiled and said, "Is it really much different from what you're already doing? Your behavior tells me you like to worry, so I'm just suggesting you put it into a different time frame." As he thought about my comment, he realized I was right: He really *wanted* to worry. And until he decided he didn't want to worry, there was nothing I could do to help him.

This is very important: *Unless we make a value judgment on our negative behavior, we will never change.*

The issue parallels the question Jesus asked the lame man at the pool of Bethesda: "Do you want to become well? [Are you really in earnest about getting well?]" (John 5:6 AMP). We must make some conscious, honest decisions about our worry. Do we like it or dislike it? Is it to our advantage or disadvantage? Is our life better with it or without it? If you're not sure, apply the techniques in this chapter and commit yourself not to worry for a period of just two weeks. Then, from your own experience, decide whether you prefer a life of worry or a life of freedom from worry.

Try a painful reminder. I've run into some very intense worriers whose thought patterns bordered on the obsessive. In a few cases I've suggested something quite radical for eliminating their negative thoughts.

One such worrier was a young man in his mid-twenties who had literally worried himself into an ulcer. I suggested he place a large, loose rubber band around his wrist. When he started to worry, he was to stretch the rubber band away from his wrist and let it go, snapping himself painfully. For him, continuing to worry was indeed painful.

The next week he came in and showed me his tender wrists. He felt he needed something radical and that it was effective. Unfortunately, in his case, it was too late. A couple of months later, half his stomach was removed.

Tell yourself to stop. During one session of a Sunday school class that I was teaching on the subject of worry, I asked participants to report on an experience I had suggested the previous week for kicking the worry out of their lives. One woman said she began the experiment Monday morning, and by Friday she felt the worry pattern that had plagued her for years was finally broken.

What accomplished this radical improvement? It was a simple method of applying God's Word to her life in a new way. I have shared this method with hundreds of people in my counseling office and with thousands in classes and seminars.

Take a blank index card and on one side write the word STOP in large, bold letters. On the other side write the complete text of Philippians 4:6-9. (I especially like the Amplified Bible rendition.) It's interesting to note that God says *He* will guard our hearts but *we* are to guard our minds. Keep the card with you at all times. Whenever you're alone and begin to worry, take the card out, hold the STOP side in front of you, and say aloud "Stop!" twice with emphasis. Then turn the card over and read the Scripture passage aloud twice with emphasis.

> Do not fret *or* have any anxiety about anything, but in every circumstance and in everything, by prayer and petition [define requests], with thanksgiving, continue to make your wants known to God. And God's peace [shall be yours, that tranquil state of a soul assured of its salvation through Christ, and so fearing nothing from God and content with its earthly lot whatever sort that is, that peace] which transcends all understanding shall garrison *and* mount guard over your hearts and minds in Christ Jesus. For the rest, brethren, whatever is true, whatever is worthy of reverence and is honorable and seemly, whatever is just, whatever is pure, whatever is lovely and lovable, whatever is kind and winsome and gracious, if there is any virtue and excellence, if there is anything worthy of praise, think on and weigh and take account of these things [fix your minds on them]. Practice what you have learned and received and heard and seen in me, and model your way of living on it, and the God of peace (of untroubled, undisturbed well-being) will be with you (AMP).

Taking the card out interrupts your thought pattern of worry. Saying the word "Stop!" further breaks your automatic habit pattern of worry. Then reading the Word of God aloud becomes the positive substitute for worry. If you are in a group of people and begin to worry, follow the same procedure, only do it silently.

The woman who shared in the class said that on the first day of her experiment she took out the card 20 times during the day. But on Friday she took it out only three times. Her words were, "For the first time in my life, I have the hope that my worrisome thinking can be chased out of my life."

Other Actions

Exercise is one of the best anti-worry responses you can use. (As long as you don't continue to worry while you are exercising!) Did you know that exercise works as an antidepressant, reduces tension, reduces frustration and anger, improves your sleep, helps your concentration, and helps keep you from being distracted? While you exercise, you can memorize Scripture, read (if you're riding a stationary bike), or pray. It can help your weight, blood pressure, and heartrate. Over the past 15 years of regular exercise, my heartrate went from 80 to 58.

Dr. Edward Hallowell, a psychiatrist, has developed an approach called EPR. It stands for Evaluate, Plan, and Remediate. If this becomes a habit, it can defeat the onslaught of many of your worries. It's an approach that turns worry into action. It's a form of plan-making. I know that some personality types aren't really into plan-making, but regardless of who we are, we can and perhaps need to do this to bring more order into our life. Here are some examples:

Perhaps you've had some shooting pains in your lower back that come and go. One day they're there, the next day they're not. But the pattern persists for several weeks. You read a couple of articles that appear to describe the same symptoms that you are having—but the outcome for the individual described was terminal cancer. After reading this your mind takes over, because the seeds of worry were planted. Now the worry intensifies. Instead of creating misery, you could do the following.

Evaluate: Say to yourself:

> This is a new condition for me. The pain is not overwhelming but annoying. I don't like the pattern it's developing. It doesn't seem to be going away on its own.

Plan: I don't know the causes or what this means. I know I avoid doctors, but the persistence of this means I need to talk to a doctor.

Remediate: You call your doctor and make an appointment.

It sounds so simple it's almost insulting. You may be thinking "That's just what I do all the time!" Great, but many worriers become immobilized and never even get to the first phase, "Evaluate."

Here's another one: You've been asked to host a meeting at your home in two days. Without thinking about the undone projects around the house, you agreed to the meeting. Just thinking about all that has to be done, as well as wanting to make a good impression, your body begins to tense up and worry begins to run through your mind. You start one task, become distracted, then go to another. Nothing is getting done except that you're getting more and more upset.

Evaluate: It's true. I've got a problem. I've been letting the house go and it is a mess. It's cluttered, and the way I'm trying to solve this isn't working. I've got to do something better than what I'm doing now.

Plan: All right, the people will probably be in just three rooms—the living room, bathroom, and kitchen. I'll concentrate on those three to clean and declutter. I'll stay in one room and one section of that room and stay until it's done. That way I can see progress.

Remediate: You take the largest room first and complete it.

Productive Worry

Did you ever consider the idea that a form of worry could be productive? I like to call it the CC *process* or *Constructive Concern*. Actually it's a preventive to worry and anxiety. I found a book written by a very successful CEO of Intel, a very successful company. Andrew Groul wrote *Only the Paranoid Survive*. It's a book which invites people to succeed. He suggests that instead of not being paranoid, be *creatively* paranoid. He suggests that we anticipate every possible alternative, learn from it, and do something about it. Don't ignore real or possible problems, but be positive about your ability to deal with the negative.[17]

Inventory your worries. Whenever worry plagues you, use some or all of the following suggestions to help you inventory your worries and plan your strategy.

1. Be sure to have your doctor give you a complete physical examination. Have him or her check your glands, vitamin deficiencies, allergies, exercise schedule, and fatigue.

2. Face your worries and admit them when they occur. Don't run from them, for they will return to haunt you. Do not worry about worrying. That just reinforces and perpetuates the problem.

3. Itemize your worries and anxieties on a sheet of paper. Be specific and complete as you describe them.

4. Write down the reasons or causes for your worry. Investigate the sources. Is there any possibility that you can eliminate the source or the cause of your worry? Have you tried? What have you tried specifically?

5. Write down the amount of time you spend each day worrying.

6. What has worrying accomplished in your life? Describe the benefits of worrying in detail.

7. Make a list of the following: a) the ways your worrying has prevented a feared situation from occurring; b) the ways your worrying increased the problem.

8. If you are nervous or jumpy, try to eliminate any sources of irritation. Stay away from them until you learn how to react differently. For example, if troubling world events worry you, don't watch so many newscasts. Use that time to relax by reading, working in the garden, or riding a bike for several miles. Avoid rushing yourself. If you worry about being late, plan to arrive at a destination early. Give yourself more time.

9. Avoid any type of fatigue—physical, emotional, or intellectual. When you are fatigued, worrisome difficulties can loom out of proportion.

10. When you do get involved in worry, is it over something that really pertains to you and your life, or does it properly belong to someone else? Remember that our fears or worries often may be disguised fears of what others think of us.

11. When a problem arises, face it and decide what you can do about it. Make a list of all of the possible solutions and decide which you think is the best one. If these are minor decisions, make them fairly quickly. Take more time for major decisions.

A worrier usually says, "I go over and over these problems and cannot decide which is best." Look at the facts, then make yourself decide. After you have made your decision, do not question or worry about your choice. Otherwise the worrying pattern erupts all over again. Practice this new pattern of making decisions.

Freedom from worry is possible! It requires that you practice the diligent application of God's Word in your life. This means repetitive behavior. If you fail, don't give up. You may have practiced worrying for many years, and now you need to practice consistently the application of Scripture over a long period in order to completely establish a new, worry-free pattern.

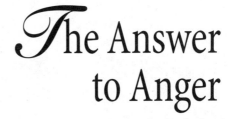

The Answer
to Anger

$\mathcal{T}$he Problem with Anger

Anger. That controversial, misunderstood word. That controversial misunderstood emotion! It affects all of us, yet continues to baffle us.

Even the so-called experts disagree. Some say, "Experience it and express it." Others say, "Disown it and repel it." But it's with us whether we like it or not. We were created with the capacity to become angry.

One dictionary calls anger "a feeling of strong displeasure." Is that your definition, or do you couch it in other terms? How would you describe it? The dictionary definition suggests that anger is manageable, that it is like so many other feelings—neither right nor wrong in itself. The problem lies in its mishandling.

Some people express their anger like a heat-seeking missile. There is no warning. No alarms sound. Everything has been calm. And then the missile explodes. The damage can include wounded feelings and distanced relationships. The recovery from the onslaught can take days or even longer.

On other occasions, anger is a snake, gliding silently and unseen through the underbrush. It may raise its head, promising a commitment, but then it disappears once more, its promise forgotten. Or the anger may slink by as a costly delay by someone who is full of weak excuses. The bite of this anger is not as blatant or devastating as the missile, but the results can be similar.

Too often we link any expression of anger with an explosion. Have you noticed some of the major synonyms used for anger? Wrath, rage, fury, hostility. These words paint the picture of anger out of control and running wild. They reflect an anger that is destructive. Some of us equate anger with our memories of the comic book and television hero "The Incredible Hulk," an out-of-control, raging beast—anger uncontrolled. On the other hand, others would like to maintain a staid emotional composure like Mr. Spock, the emotionless Vulcan on the Star Trek TV series. He never allowed himself to be angry.

Often anger begins slowly. It starts as a slight arousal, a feeling of discomfort. We begin to notice changes in our body, especially a feeling of tension. Our pulse rate increases, and there is a surge of adrenaline. You've felt it, and so have I. It's been that way throughout all of history.

The Many Faces of Anger

But anger wears many faces. Moses was livid with anger at the Hebrew people when they set up idol worship. With the energy provided by his anger he was able to regain control of the people. David was consumed with anger when Nathan told him about the rich man stealing from the poor man. He used this anger to face his own pride and admit his own sin. Anger can be used in a creative way to resolve major social problems.

In the early chapters of the Gospel of Mark we find the Pharisees looking for ways to find fault with Christ. Once Christ entered a synagogue and noticed a man with a withered hand. The Pharisees watched His every move to see if Christ would heal the man. Christ turned to the man and said, "Rise and come forward!" He turned to the Pharisees and asked, "Is it lawful on the Sabbath to do good or to do harm, to save a life or to kill?" They wouldn't answer Him (see Mark 3:1-5 NASB).

"After looking around at them with anger, grieved at their hardness of heart, He said to the man, 'Stretch out your hand.' And he stretched it out, and his hand was restored." Christ felt and expressed anger at the injustice of the Pharisees. He was frustrated by the fact that they held their rigid orthodoxy to man-made rule as more important than the suffering of another man.

Elizabeth Skoglund said,

> Christ Himself was slow to anger with the woman caught in adultery because He knew her heart, and He reacted quickly against her accusers because He also knew their inner thoughts. He showed anger at the disciples when they tried to keep the children from Him, and yet He was tender when the multitudes pressed against Him. In violent anger He chased the money changers out of the temple, but He showed only a weary disappointment when the disciples slept while He prayed in the Garden of Gethsemane.
>
> The most significant example of slowness to anger in the history of mankind was exhibited two thousand years ago by Jesus. Christ, the God-man crucified by the caprice of a mob and the weakness of those in authority, prayed with agonized genuineness, "Father, forgive these people, for they don't know what they are doing" (Luke 23:34 TLB). His profound comprehension of the significance of what he was doing contrasted with the total ignorance of the crowds. His sensitivity of them and their plight helped make Him slow to anger indeed.[18]

Jesus experienced anger and felt free to let it show. He clearly and *constructively* expressed His anger.

An injustice involves the violation of that which is moral or right, the rights of another person, or your own personal rights. There are examples of acts of unfairness and injustice all around us.

Anger is a frequent and potentially healthy response to injustice. Abraham Lincoln, Gandhi, and Martin Luther King Jr., are all examples of men in whom injustice could trigger an angry response. They also provide examples of ways in which the energy from anger can be used for good. When our anger is channeled into righteous indignation it can help us identify the injustice. Then we can reach out in unselfish acts to the downtrodden and mistreated to right the wrong, to build up rather than tear down, to attack the problem and not the person.

Positive Anger

A mother who first cried and then became upset about her son's death caused by a drunk driver organized MADD (Mothers Against Drunk Driving). Her anger, put to positive use, has created an organization that now promotes legislation and awareness programs to remove drunk drivers from the nation's roads.

Anger can be used positively and creatively in many ways. For example, anger is a part of the grieving process following a loss.

Here are several ways in which anger has been used positively:

- A relative of an accident victim *convinced* the hospital chaplain staff to establish new and improved procedures for helping the survivors of sudden accidental deaths.

- A parent *proposed* that warning signs be posted at a pond where his son drowned to help reduce similar accidental incidents.

- A grandmother *requested* that parents of cancer victims be provided printed information about cancer as well as the location of support groups.

- An adult son who lost his elderly father *organized* programs for a local convalescent home.

- A young mother who lost her preschool age daughter *solicited* toy contributions to give to a local pediatric ward.

Notice the action words alone, which reflect how these people not only redirected their anger but also brought relief and a sense of control to their lives: convinced, proposed, requested, organized, and solicited.[19]

The Problem with Anger

Anger doesn't wear a happy face but an ugly face. Consider some of the destructive results of this emotion. People seem to go to extremes in their demonstration of anger, either outwardly or inwardly. Turn it outward too much, and it destroys others. Turn it inward too much, and it destroys us.

Not only did Cain misuse this emotion, but so did Esau, Saul, the Pharisees, Attila the Hun, Adolf Hitler, and certain other rulers in most of the countries of the world. Our history is a tragic drama of hostility and domination.

Did you know that anger is a motivator? It can motivate you to hate, wound, damage, annihilate, despise, scorn, loathe, vilify, curse, ruin, and demolish. When we're angry we might ridicule, get even with, laugh at, humiliate, shame, criticize, bawl out, fight, crush, offend, or bully another person. All of these do very little to build relationships.

Consider some of the words and phrases people use to describe the experience and expressions of anger:

aggravated	despise	huffy	offended
agitated	disdain	hurt	provoked
annoyed	disgusted	irked	repulsed
animosity	enraged	incensed	resentful
aroused	exasperated	ill-tempered	riled
begrudge	frustrated	ill will	sarcastic
bitter	fume	irritated	scorned
bristle	furious	infuriated	spiteful
burned up	grieved	inflamed	steamed
catty	grumpy	jealous	touchy
criticize	grouchy	mad	vexed
cool	hateful	mean	vicious
cranky	hostile	miffed	wounded
cross	hot	moody	wrath

The first time we see the effects of anger in Scripture, they're very destructive. "But on Cain and his offering he did not look with favor. So Cain was very angry, and his face was downcast. Then the LORD said to Cain, 'Why are you angry?'" (Genesis 4:5,6).

Cain was angry at his brother because Abel's sacrifice was acceptable and his own was not. Inwardly Cain experienced anger, and the result was murder (Genesis 4:8). Cain was alienated from his brother, from other people, and from God. His anger led to murder and to extreme loneliness.

Almost everything in life has a price tag. Go into any store, and rarely will you find anything that is free. Purchasing a new car may give us a feeling of elation, comfort, and prestige, but it costs. Expressing our anger can be a relief, and it can influence or even control a situation, but it too has a price tag. Some of the costs may be obvious, such as a strained relationship (resistance or withdrawal of others when we come near them). Or it could be a tension-filled marital relationship, with spouses who are now combatants rather than lovers. Even though there are personal physiological costs to anger, the greatest price to be paid is in our interpersonal relationships.

Anger has its place, since it can sometimes be constructive, but usually it's destructive. Our anger carelessly expressed will override the love, care, and appreciation that creates close relationships. The person who has a reputation for anger is soon given a wide berth. Indeed, the book of Proverbs recommends: "Make no friendships with a man given to anger, and with a wrathful man do not associate, lest you learn his ways and get yourself into a snare" (22:24,25 AMP).

Those are strong words. But the Scripture is describing a hothead, a person who fires up at the drop of a hat.

Anger erects barriers. Anger leads to aggression—it doesn't reduce it. Each expression of anger adds to the stockpile of fuel.

Anger can be a very upsetting emotion. You may be afraid of your own anger because you have seen people totally out of control with this emotion. They didn't just experience anger, they raged. Perhaps you believe that healthy people don't have anger. Or perhaps you feel that you don't have the right to be angry at others.

The Bible and Anger

The Word of God has much to say about anger, and it uses a number of words to describe the various types of anger. In the Old Testament the word for anger actually meant "nostril" or "nose." (In ancient Hebrew psychology the nose was thought to be the seat of anger.) The phrase "slow to anger" literally means "long of nose." Synonyms used in the Old Testament for anger include ill-humor and rage (Esther 1:12), overflowing rage and fury (Amos 1:11), and indignation (Jeremiah 15:17). The emotion of anger can be the subject of Scripture even though the exact word is not present. Anger can be implied through words such as revenge, cursing, jealousy, snorting, trembling, shouting, raving, and grinding the teeth.

Several words are used for anger in the New Testament. It is important to note the distinction between these words. Many people have concluded that Scripture contradicts itself because in one verse we are taught not to be angry and in another we are admonished to "be angry and sin not." Which is correct and which should we follow?

One of the words used most often for anger in the New Testament is *thumas*. It describes anger as a turbulent commotion or a boiling agitation of feelings. This type of anger blazes up into a sudden explosion. It is an outburst from inner indignation and is similar to a match which quickly ignites into a blaze but then burns out rapidly. This type of anger is mentioned 20 times in passages such as Ephesians 4:31 and Galatians 5:20. We are to control this type of anger.

Another type of anger, mentioned only three times in the New Testament (and never in a positive sense), is *parogismos*. This is anger that has been provoked. It is characterized by irritation, exasperation, or embitterment.

"Do not ever let your wrath (your exasperation, your fury or indignation) last until the sun goes down" (Ephesians 4:26 AMP).

"Again I ask, Did Israel not understand? [Did the Jews have no warning that the Gospel was to go forth to the Gentiles, to all the earth?] First, there is Moses who says, I will make you jealous of those who are not a nation; with a foolish nation I will make you angry" (Romans 10:19 AMP).

The most common New Testament word for anger is *orge*. It is used 45 times and means a more settled and long-lasting attitude which is slower in its onset but more enduring. It often includes revenge. This kind of anger is similar to coals on a barbecue slowly warming to red and then white hot and holding this temperature until the cooking is done.

There are two exceptions where this word is used and revenge is not included in its meaning. Mark 3:5 records Jesus as having looked upon the Pharisees with anger.

Ephesians 4:26 tells us to "be angry and sin not" (KJV). This is one of the passages (along with Mark 3:5) where anger is legitimate. The word "angry" in this verse means an anger which is an abiding and settled habit of the mind, and which is aroused under certain conditions. There is no revenge. You are aware of this kind of anger and it is under control. There is a legitimate reason for this anger. Your reasoning powers are involved, and when careful reason is present, anger such as this is proper. The Scriptures not only permit it but on some occasions *demand it!* Perhaps this sounds strange to those who have thought for years that anger is all wrong. But the Word of God does state that *we are to be angry!*

Paul actually commended the Corinthians in one place for their aroused indignation against the believer who had married his own mother. (See 2 Corinthians 7:11.) This is righteous anger. It is not sinful when it is properly directed. Such anger must be an abiding, settled attitude of righteous indignation against sin, coupled with appropriate action.

Righteous Anger

There are *three main characteristics* of righteous anger. First it must be *controlled*. It is not a heated, unrestrained passion. Even if the cause is legitimate and is directed at an injustice, uncontrolled anger can cause an error in judgment and increase the difficulty. The mind must be in control of the emotions so that the ability to reason is not lost. "Be angry and sin not." Perhaps the way this is accomplished is related to the scriptural teaching in Proverbs 14:29 and 16:32 to be "slow to anger" (NASB). This kind of anger is not a direct result of immediate frustration.

Second, *there must be no hatred, malice, or resentment.* Anger that harbors a counterattack only complicates the situation. Perhaps our best example of how to respond is Jesus' reaction to the injustices delivered against Him.

> When he was reviled and insulted, He did not revile or offer insult in return; [when] He was abused and suffered, He made not threats [of vengeance]; but He trusted [Himself and everything] to Him who judges fairly (I Peter 2:23 AMP).

> Beloved, never avenge yourselves, but leave the way open for [God's] wrath; for it is written, Vengeance is Mine, I will repay [requite], says the Lord (Romans 12:19 AMP).

The final characteristic of righteous anger is that *its motivation is unselfish.* When the motivation is selfish, pride and resentment are usually involved. Anger should be directed not at the wrong done to oneself but at the injustice done to others.

The basic overall theme of Scripture concerning anger is that it will be a part of life. It is not to be denied, but is to be controlled. Certain types of anger are not healthy and should be put away. Anger should be aroused against definite injustices and then used properly.

What about the type of anger that you experience? What is it like? How would you classify it as you read these definitions? Take a few moments right now and try to think of some examples of each of these types of anger in your own life. Write down the situation and circumstances and describe the results of this anger. Describe how you felt at the time and the reaction of others to you.

Anger can be constructive. Believe it or not, anger is a gift from God. It can be used for good purposes, if it is expressed properly. And when the energy from this emotion is constructively redirected, you benefit from it.

5

*U*nderstanding Your Anger

How can anger be beneficial rather than destructive? In what ways can this unwelcome and potentially destructive emotion be considered a gift to be used rather than a missile to be avoided at all costs? There are certain facts that help us to understand anger's positive potential.

God has anger, and because we were made in His image we have anger too. It is not an evil emotion. Nor is anger in itself a destructive emotion. Nor is it always dangerous. Unfortunately, many people confuse the emotion of anger with the way some people choose to *express* that emotion. Many people confuse anger with aggression. Anger is not the same as aggression. Anger is an emotion, while aggression is an action.

When we don't understand our anger and allow it to get out of control, it can lead to aggressive behaviors that are sinful, dangerous, destructive, and even deadly. But the *emotion itself* of anger isn't the problem. The real problem is the *mismanagement and misunderstanding of the emotion*. The problem is the emotional immaturity of the individual who allows himself or herself to be controlled by the anger-energy.

We can't always control when or how we experience anger, but with God's help we can learn to control how we choose to interpret and express that emotion. Because God has made us rational creatures, we are free to choose how we will respond to external events. In fact, we have more control than we give ourselves credit for. Often, however, our past experiences, memories, and patterns of response tend to hinder us from exercising this control. Yet with understanding, time, and practice we can overcome these influences and develop constructive and healthy responses to our anger.

Anger: A Secondary Emotion

Anger is a warning sign, a clue to underlying attitudes. Anger is designed to help us detect improper and potentially destructive attitudes.

Anger may be the first emotion we are aware of, but it is rarely the first emotion we experience in a particular situation. The emotions that most frequently precede anger are *fear, hurt,* or *frustration.* Not only are they painful, but they also drain us of energy and increase our sense of vulnerability.

At an early age many of us learned that anger can divert our attention from these more painful emotions. If I get angry I can avoid or at least minimize my pain. Perhaps I can even influence or change the source of my anger. It doesn't take us long to learn that it's easier to feel anger than it is to feel pain. Anger provides an increase of energy and can decrease our sense of vulnerability.

Unfortunately, the vast majority of people never realize that anger, like depression, is simply a form of message that we are sending to ourselves.

When a person experiences *hurt* such as rejection, criticism, or physical or emotional pain, a very normal reaction is anger. We strike back and counterattack that which we feel is causing the pain.

Remember when Jesus looked at the Pharisees with anger? The passage stated that He was "grieved at the hardness of their heart" (Mark 3:5 NASB). He was hurt at that time.

Another cause of anger is *frustration*. (More about this later.)

Fear also causes anger. When we are afraid of something, we often do not act afraid, but instead become angry. For some reason anger is more comfortable than fear. Perhaps it is because we are on the offensive rather than the defensive. When you are afraid and act in anger you confuse others around you. You are not telling them what you are really feeling inside, so all they can do is respond to your anger. Unfortunately, in most cases anger begets anger.

Take the example of the husband who is home every night from work at 6:00. One night he is late. The time gets to be 6:40, 7:00, and 7:30 but there's not a word from him. All this time his wife is becoming increasingly worried, concerned, and fearful. She begins thinking that something awful has happened to him. Finally, about eight o'clock he comes in and announces that he is home and asks if there is any dinner left. Instead of going to him and sharing her fear and concern, she responds, "Well, where have you been? You sure are inconsiderate not letting me know that you were going to be late." You can probably think of similar situations.

When you are angry, ask yourself these questions: Do I feel hurt? Am I experiencing frustration over something? What am I frustrated about? Am I afraid of something at this time? Write these on a 3 x 5 card and carry it with you to remind you.

If you are with another person who is angry, instead of becoming angry at his or her anger, perhaps with sensitivity and compassion you could ask him, "Are you feeling hurt over something right now? Are you frustrated about a situation at this time? Are you in some way afraid?"

The Many Disguises of Anger

We do not always recognize anger because it crops up in ways other than a strong physical or verbal response. What are some of the most common disguises anger can take? When we begrudge, scorn, insult, and disdain others, or when we feel annoyed, offended, bitter, fed up, or repulsed, we are probably experiencing some form of anger. Some people are angry when they become sarcastic, tense, or cross; or when they feel frustration, exasperation, or wrath. Anger can also manifest itself as criticism, silence, intimidation, hypochondria, numerous petty complaints, depression, gossip, and blame.

Even behaviors such as stubbornness, halfhearted efforts, forgetfulness, and laziness can be evidence of an angry spirit.

Have you ever used or seen any of the following responses?

- Joking—you hide intentional painful remarks with humor or ridicule.
- Acting confused—you pretend you don't understand another person or you're confused.
- Appearing tired—you act tired to avoid contact with another person, agreeing with everything. You make passive comments with a certain tone of voice like "Sure . . ." "Whatever . . ." an so on.
- Not hearing—you pretend you didn't hear what the other person said.
- Being clumsy—you "accidentally" break something on purpose.

We call these passive aggressive responses. And if they're used on you they're very irritating! An important part of learning how to make our anger work for us is to be able to identify the many masks or disguises of anger.

Admitting Your Anger

When is the last time you admitted that you were angry? What did it feel like? Did you feel a little ashamed or embarrassed? Have you ever wanted to stand up in front of your congregation on Sunday and admit you're angry? I don't think so! One reason anger is so difficult for most of us to deal with is that we are not comfortable admitting that we are angry.

This is especially true for many Christians who believe that all anger is a sign of spiritual immaturity and weakness. When they do acknowledge their anger they usually describe themselves as being discouraged, frustrated, sad, worried, depressed, annoyed, or irritated. Have you ever done this? That is much easier than looking someone straight in the eyes and saying, "I am angry."

What makes it even more difficult is that often the source of our anger has been something silly or insignificant. We've all experienced anger over little things. At one time or another every one of us has overreacted to what was clearly something small.

Your Three Choices

Once a person discovers he is angry, how can he deal with that anger? What choices are available to him?

There are three basic ways to deal with anger.

One way is to *repress* it—to never admit that you're angry, to simply ignore its presence. This repression is often unconscious, but it is *not healthy!* Repressing anger is like placing a wastebasket full of paper in a closet and setting fire to it. The fire will either burn itself out or else set the whole house on fire. The energy produced by anger cannot be destroyed. It must be converted or directed into another channel.

One outlet for repressed anger is accidents. Perhaps you have met people who are accident-prone. Unfortunately, their accidents may involve other people as well as themselves. A man who is angry may slam a door on his own hand or someone else's. He may wash windows for his wife when he would rather be watching a game on TV and put his hand through the window. His driving may manifest his anger when he "accidentally" runs over the rosebushes.

Repressed anger can easily take its toll on your body by giving you a vicious headache. Your gastrointestinal system— that 30-foot tube extending from the mouth to the rectum— reacts adversely to repressed anger. You may experience difficulty in swallowing, nausea and vomiting, gastric ulcer, constipation, or diarrhea. The most common cause of ulcerative colitis is repressed anger. Repressed anger can affect the skin through pruritus, itching, and neurodermatitis. Respiratory disorders such as asthma are also common effects, and the role of anger in coronary thrombosis is fairly well accepted.

At some time and in some way the ignored or buried emotion of anger will express itself—physically, psychologically, or spiritually. In other words, there will be a resurrection of your anger, but you won't be in charge of it.

What are some of the long-term costs of ignoring our anger? A 12-year longitudinal study of 10,000 people revealed that those who repressed anger were more than twice as likely to die of heart disease as those who expressed anger in healthy ways. A 25-year study showed that people with high hostility scores had higher incidence of heart disease; they were also five times more likely to die by age 50 from all causes of disease than their low-scoring counterparts. Other research over a 20-year period correlated higher hostility scores not only with increased rates of coronary heart disease but also with increased incidence of cancer, accidents, and suicide.[20]

Significant work has been done with cancer victims. The results of the research suggest that there is a cancer-prone personality, that certain combinations of traits make some people especially vulnerable to cancer. Some of these characteristics include a tendency to hold resentment and an inability or unwillingness to forgive.

In his book *Free for the Taking*, missionary Joseph Cooke tells how he tried to suppress his anger:

> Squelching our feelings never pays. In fact, it's rather like plugging up a steam vent in a boiler. When the steam is stopped in one place, it will come out somewhere else. Either that or the whole business will blow up in your face. And bottled-up feelings are just the same. If you bite down

your anger, for example, it often comes out in another form that is more difficult to deal with. It changes into sullenness, self-pity, depression, or snide, cutting remarks. . . .

Not only may bottled-up emotions come out sideways in various unpleasant forms; they also may build up pressure until they simply have to burst, and when they do, someone is almost always bound to get hurt. I remember that for years of my life, I worked to bring my emotions under control. Over and over again, as they cropped up, I would master them in my attempt to achieve what looked like a gracious . . . Christian spirit. Eventually I had nearly everybody fooled, even in a measure my own wife. But it was all a fake. . . . The time came when the whole works blew up in my face, in an emotional breakdown. All the things that had been buried so long came out in the open. Frankly, there was no healing, no recovery, no building a new life for me until all those feelings were sorted out, and until I learned to know them for what they were, accept them, and find some way of expressing them honestly and nondestructively.[21]

Anger and depression are among the most common problems of those who seek professional counseling. Furthermore, they are not new problems. Throughout biblical history great men of God labored under these emotions. Jonah is perhaps the classic example. He was sent by God to warn the people of Nineveh about their sinfulness. He completed this task successfully to the point where the King of Nineveh turned from his sin and commanded his people to do likewise. In turn God "abandoned his plan to destroy them, and didn't carry it through" (Jonah 3:10 TLB).

The biblical record goes on to say, "This change of plans made Jonah very angry. He complained to the Lord about it: 'This is exactly what I thought you'd do, Lord, when I was there in my own country and you first told me to come here. . . . For I knew you were a gracious god, merciful, slow to get angry, and full of kindness; I knew how easily you could cancel your plans for destroying these people. Please kill me, Lord; I'd rather be dead than alive. . . .' Then the Lord said, 'Is it right to be *angry* about *this?*' So Jonah went out and sat sulking on the east side of the city" (Jonah 4:1-5 TLB).

However, all does not go well with Jonah; depressed, he sits under a vine. The vine dries, and the heat from the sun becomes intense. Then in a last recorded dialogue with God, Jonah states, "It is right for me to be angry enough to die" (Jonah 4:9 TLB). Anger turned outward made Jonah seek the cooling comfort of the vine, but then his anger turned inward and became depression. At one point Jonah was content just to sit and "hole up," and at another point he wished for—indeed asked for—death.

While depression and anger are not usually linked this clearly in Scripture, they are presented as acceptable emotions when handled responsibly.[22]

A second way to handle anger is to *suppress* it. A person is aware of his anger but chooses to hold it in and not let others know he is angry. In some situations this may be wise, but eventually the anger needs to be recognized and drained away in a healthy manner. But the person who *always* stuffs anger away is a sad case. The constant effort of keeping it in is an incredible waste of energy.

Though their cheerful, smiling exteriors make it seem otherwise, *stuffers* are usually very unhappy people. Some stuffers literally stuff themselves by eating enormous amounts of food, partly as a way of punishing themselves for the "sin of anger" (as they perceive it).

Often a person chooses to suppress his anger when the one with whom he is angry could react with more force or authority. For example, an employer calls in one of his employees. He angrily confronts him about some alleged problem. The employee feels his own anger rising but realizes that if he expresses his anger to his boss he could lose his job. So he suppresses his anger—until he arrives home.

His wife greets him when he walks in the door and he replies with an angry snarl. This surprises her. She either reacts by snapping back at him or by following her husband's previous example and suppressing her anger. But then their teenage son walks in and she vents her pent-up anger upon the unsuspecting boy. He takes out his anger on the younger brother, who in turn kicks the dog, who bites the cat, who scratches the three-year-old, who takes out her frustration by pulling off the head of her Barbie doll!

This simple process of directing your anger on a less-threatening person is called *displacement*. It may help you for a moment, but it can set up a long-lasting chain of events that infects the lives of others like an epidemic.

Guilt is another reason for displacing anger. If you are furious with your mother but believe that it is wrong to get angry with one's mother, you may find yourself exploding at other older women. Or you may use displacement to avoid humiliating yourself. You're traveling with your husband and trying to make mileage on a particular day. You take a wrong turn and go 50 miles in the wrong direction. You then project the blame onto your husband and accuse him of misguiding you. (Of course we all know that men won't ask for directions!)

Instead it's better to deal with the problem directly. If you disagree with your employer over office procedures, the solution is not to complain to your wife or to another employee, but to talk with the boss and attempt to resolve the problem. If this is not practical, then you must put up with the situation and find other constructive outlets for your anger when it arises. The ideal solution is to practice various responses to the cause of your frustration.

If the cause for your anger is not legitimate, the problem is within you. If you get angry with your wife because she does not cook meals the way your mother did, then you had better begin by recognizing that your wife is not your mother! Allow her to develop her own cooking skills and try some new recipes. Then learn to compromise on some of your expectations.

How can intense negative feelings be resolved or ventilated without blasting away at the offender? Are there ways of releasing pent-up emotions?

You could:

- Make the irritation a matter of prayer.
- Explain your negative feelings to a mature and understanding third party who can advise and lead you.
- Go to an offender and show a spirit of love and forgiveness.

Understand that God often permits the most frustrating and agitating events to occur in order to teach us patience and help us grow.

Suppressing anger does have some merit, however, especially if it helps you relax, cool down, and begin to act in a rational manner. The Word of God has something to say about this type of suppression:

> He who is slow to anger has great understanding, but he who is hasty of spirit exposes and exalts his folly (Proverbs 14:29 AMP). This man is one who actually suppresses strife in the beginning so it doesn't break out.

> He who is slow to anger is better than the mighty, and he who rules his own spirit than he who takes a city (Proverbs 16:32 AMP).

> Good sense makes a man restrain his anger, and it is his glory to overlook a transgression or an offense (Proverbs 19:11 AMP).

> A [self-confident] fool utters all his anger, but a wise man keeps it back and stills it" (Proverbs 29:11 AMP). This passage means that the person does not give unbridled license to his anger but sort of hushes it up and puts it in the background. It also means that anger is overcome.

I [Nehemiah] was very angry when I heard their cry and these words. I thought it over and then rebuked the nobles and officials (Nehemiah 5:6,7 AMP). One version translates this verse as "I consulted with myself."

The individual who practices and exerts self-control will find that his anger level actually decreases. He will not become as angry as if he were to simply cut loose with his first reaction. A calm consideration of the cause for the anger and the results will help you handle the situation properly.

Expressing your anger is a third way to handle it. Some people think you should express exactly how you feel no matter what or who is involved. They feel this is psychologically healthy and necessary in order to live a balanced life.

There are many different ways to express anger. The worst way is to react with violent passion—yelling harsh words and swearing, all with tremendous emotion.

The way you express your anger is a form of communication. The more successful you are in communicating in a certain way, the greater the possibility you'll continue in that way. If you have been reinforced for being angry (gotten what you wanted), then you will most likely continue to express it in that way.

The expression of anger does bring results. However, research shows that "letting out or fully expressing" your anger in a cathartic way doesn't reduce your frustration, but often leaves you more uptight instead. And angry outbursts invite retaliation.

Expressing anger means you're more likely to do it again in the same way. You may let it out, but it doesn't stay out. When you express anger you are not purging yourself of it but actually practicing it. Letting it all out may actually let it all back in. It moves you further from others rather than drawing you closer.[23]

This *can* bring results, but not the kind you want. If you are allowed the freedom to react in this way, shouldn't the other person have the freedom to react to you in the same way?

But you can also express your anger by riding your bike around the block, digging in the garden for an hour, or beating on a stuffed pillow. Some of these people are called *doers*. You can write down exactly how you feel when you get angry, especially if it is difficult to verbalize your feelings. These methods may sound strange but they should not be discounted. They have been used to help many people overcome their difficulties with anger.

If both you and your spouse are angry, it is better, if you are working it off physically, to do it separately. For some reason the anger disappears faster.

What habitual *doers* need to keep in mind, however, is that while pounding a tennis ball, polishing a floor, or sewing an exciting seam may make them feel better, these activities are seldom directly related to the source of the anger.

Everyone can and probably should be a *doer* some of the time, but if your only way of handling anger is to escape into physical activity, ask yourself the following questions from time to time: At whom am I angry and why? How can I change things and feel better?

6

$\mathscr{A}$nger Under Control

One of the best reasons for not getting angry is that anger actually prevents a person from solving problems. It is not a solution to frustration but a reaction to frustration. If your spouse is after you to work on your marriage relationship or spend more time with the children, the solution is to talk about it. Find out how your spouse really feels, and do as much as you can to enhance your relationship.

If you don't like your working conditions, what can you do? You can either attempt to improve the working atmosphere, learn to live with an undesirable (but not intolerable) situation, or look for another job. Getting angry will not bring about positive, lasting improvements in which all parties are satisfied.

Frustration and Fire

One way of dealing with anger is to approach it from the perspective of frustration. If anger has been brought about by frustration, it will have a tendency to disappear if the frustration is removed. If a child is having a fit because he can't have a candy bar, he will tend to control himself if the parent succumbs to his antics and gives him the candy. If a man is angry because a planned fishing trip may be suddenly canceled, he will tend to quiet down if he is able to go on that trip. If you are angry because a child is not responding to your attempts at discipline, your anger will subside when he begins behaving.

The point to remember is that the energy of anger does not have to be unleashed in a manner that will hurt or destroy. Instead it can be used in a constructive manner to *eliminate* the frustration. If the original frustration cannot be eliminated, many people learn to accept substitute goals and thereby find nearly as much and sometimes even greater satisfaction.

Reacting with anger is like pouring gasoline on a fire that is already blazing. A chemical retardant would be far better. Proverbs 15:1 illustrates an appropriate response: "A soft answer turneth away wrath, but grievous words stir up anger" (KJV).

This verse does not say that the other person's anger will be turned away *immediately*, but in time it will happen. Remember that you will have to plan your verbal and nonverbal response to this person well in advance and even practice it if you expect it to happen. If you wait until you are in the heat of the altercation, you will not (and cannot because of physical changes) be able to change your old angry way of reacting. Visualizing and practicing the scriptural teaching in advance prepares you to make the proper response.

Why do you become angry at your family members when they don't respond to you? Why do you get angry at the kids when they don't pick up their room, mow the lawn, or dry the dishes properly? Anger expressed by yelling at a son who does not mow the lawn carefully does not teach him how to do it correctly. Angry words directed to a sloppy daughter do not teach her how to be neat. Step-by-step instruction (even if it has been given before) can help solve the problem.

Another result of anger is that you become a carrier of a very infectious germ—anger itself. If you respond in anger, others around you can easily catch the germ. If you become angry at your spouse, don't be surprised if he or she responds in like manner. You gave your husband or wife an example to follow. Your spouse is responsible for his or her own emotional responses, but you still modeled the response. Perhaps if you respond with a kind but firm reply your spouse could follow this example.

Reducing Your Frustration

I hear people in my office and in my seminars say to me again and again, "Norm, I don't want to talk in an angry way to others, especially my family, but something just comes over me and I let it rip! There's a limit to what I can take. I know I really love them, but sometimes I don't like them very much. I don't know what to do to change."

I usually respond with a question: "When you feel frustrated and angry with your family members, what do you focus on: how they act at what you said or how you would like them to act?"

They usually reply, "Oh, I keep mulling over what I didn't like and my destructive comments. I relive it again and again and beat up on myself for hurting them."

"Do you realize that by rehearsing your failures you are programming yourself to repeat them?" I ask.

They usually respond with a puzzled look. But it's true. When you spend so much time thinking about what you *shouldn't* have done, you reinforce it. Furthermore, spending all your time and energy mentally rehashing your failures keeps you from formulating what you really *want* to do. Redirecting your time and energy toward a solution will make a big difference in how you communicate with anyone. Focus your attention on how you want to respond to your frustrations and you *will* experience change!

Let's consider several steps you can take to reduce your frustration and to curb words that you don't want to express.

The first step is to find someone with whom you can share your concerns and develop an accountability relationship. Select someone who will be willing to pray with you and check up on you regularly to see how you are doing. If you are working through these steps as a couple, ask another couple to keep you accountable. We all need the support and assistance of others.

You also need to be honest and accountable to yourself and others about changes you want to make. Take a sheet of paper and respond in writing to the following questions. Then share your responses with your prayer partner.

- How do you feel about becoming frustrated? Be specific. How do you feel about getting angry? There are some people who enjoy their frustration and anger. It gives them an adrenaline rush and a feeling of power. Does this description fit you in any way?

- When you are frustrated, do you want to be in control of your response or to be spontaneous? In other words, do you want to decide what to do or just let your feelings take you where they want to go?

- If you want to stay in control, how much time and energy are you willing to spend to make this happen? For change to occur, the motivational level needs to remain both constant and high.

- When you are bothered by something that someone else does, how would you like to respond? What would you like to say at that time? Be specific.

There is a reason why God inspired men to write the Scriptures and why He preserved His words through the centuries for us: *God's guidelines for life are the best.* Regardless of what you may have experienced or been taught in the past, God's plan works!

Write out each of the following verses from Proverbs on separate index cards:

> Reckless words pierce like a sword, but the tongue of the wise brings healing (12:18).

A patient man has great understanding, but a quick-tempered man displays folly (14:29).

Better a patient man than a warrior, a man who controls his temper than one who takes a city (16:32).

Add to your card file other Scriptures you discover which relate to frustration and anger. Read these verses aloud morning and evening for three weeks and you will own them.

You will be able to change only if you plan to change. Your intentions may be good, but once the frustration-anger sequence kicks into gear, your ability to think clearly is limited.

Identify in advance what you want to say when you begin to feel frustrated. Be specific. Write out your responses and read them aloud to yourself and to your prayer partner. In my counseling office I often have clients practice their new responses on me, and I attempt to respond as the other person. By practicing on me they are able to refine their statements, eliminate their anxiety or feelings of discomfort, and gain confidence for their new approach. Your spouse or prayer partner could assist you this way.

Begin training yourself to *delay* your verbal and behavioral responses when you recognize that you are frustrated. The Proverbs repeatedly admonish us to be *slow* to anger. You must slow down your responses if you want to change any habits of words you have cultivated over the years. When we allow frustration and anger to be expressed unhindered, they are like a runaway locomotive. You need to catch them before they gather momentum so you can switch the tracks and steer them in the right direction.[24]

One helpful way to change direction is to use a *trigger word*. Whenever you feel frustration and anger rising within you, remind yourself to slow down and gain control by saying something to yourself like "stop," "think," "control," and so on. Those are words that will help you switch gears and put your new plan into action.

One of the approaches I often suggest to defuse a frustrating situation is this: Mentally give the other person permission to be involved in the behavior which frustrates you. The permission-giving approach defuses your frustration and gives you time to implement a levelheaded plan.

I'm not suggesting that you emotionally give up and allow others to do anything they want to do. There are some behaviors which are highly detrimental and require a direct response.

Many people are skeptical when I suggest the permission-giving strategy. But they often come back after trying it and report amazing results. One person said, "Norm, the first time I heard your suggestion, I thought you were crazy. But I tried it. I discovered that I was less frustrated. My posture was less rigid, and I was more relaxed as I dealt with that person."

Your inner conversation—also called self-talk—is where your frustrations are either tamed or inflamed. What you say to others and how you behave is determined by how you talk to yourself about their behaviors and responses. Self-talk is the words and ideas you think to yourself. In fact, your most powerful emotions—anger, depression, guilt, worry—as well as your self-image as a person are initiated and fed by your inner conversations. Changing your inner conversation is essential to keeping your frustrations from erupting into wounding words.

There will be times when you know in advance that you're in a situation which may lead to someone getting angry—you. If you listen to what you usually say in a similar situation, you will be able to identify two things: what it is that generates your anger and what you can do to adjust your attitude. You will also discover your expectations so that the situation can be less anger-producing. Here are some samples of anger-reducing self-talk:

- I won't take what is said or done personally.

- No matter what happens, I know I can learn to control my frustrations and anger. I have this capability because of the presence of Jesus in my life and His strength.

- I am going to stay calm and in control.

- I will respond to statements that usually trigger me with statements like "That's interesting," "I'll think about that," or "Could you tell me more about this situation?"

- I don't have to allow this situation to bother me.

- If I begin to get upset I will take some deep breaths, slow down, delay my responses, and purposely speak softer.[25]

God's Word has a lot to say about how we think. If you have difficulty with negative inner conversations, I suggest that you write out the following Scriptures on index cards and begin reading them aloud to yourself every morning and evening: Isaiah 26:3; Romans 8:6,7; 2 Corinthians 10:5; Ephesians 4:24; Philippians 4:6-9; 1 Peter 1:13.

If you approach these steps thinking, "This will never work," you have set yourself up for failure. Instead you could think, "I'm taking positive steps toward resolving my frustration and anger. This will really make a difference in my relationship with others. I know my communication will improve as I take these steps of growth."

To help you to develop a positive attitude, take a minute to list the advantages of being frustrated. Compare the two lists. Which results do you want? You are more likely to achieve these results by following the steps above.

What You Can Do

In any expression of anger between two people, you are responsible for your own anger. The other person is responsible for his. Anger does happen in our families.

You can project the anger onto the other person and hold him or her responsible for the way you feel and act. But this demands that he be the one to change. Holding him or her responsible is a protective response on your part. It says, "I have been victimized by you." But if you focus on yourself and take responsibility for the way you feel, there is a greater chance of resolving an issue.

Instead of saying, "You made me angry," tell him or her "You acted in this way, and I *felt* angry because of the way you behaved."

As your own anger begins to escalate, use the interruption approach on yourself. Remember that earlier in this book we identified the three basic causes of anger as fear, hurt, and frustration. Anger is the secondary response to any of these three.

If anger is a problem for you, keep a 3 x 5 card with you. On one side print the word *STOP!* in large letters. On the other side print the following questions:

> Am I experiencing hurt over something right now?
> Am I in some way afraid?
> Am I frustrated over something at this time?

The minute you begin to experience rising anger, take out the card, read the word *STOP!* (out loud if it's appropriate), and then turn the card over. Read and respond to the three questions. Slowing down your anger response and identifying the cause will help you resolve the issue. You can still assume responsibility for choosing to respond in a way that will help defuse the other person rather than fuel the interchange.

Other People's Anger

It is important for you to clarify in your own mind why you want to reduce the amount of anger in the other person. You may simply find anger distasteful. Or you could be afraid that it might get out of hand. Or you might feel that it prolongs disagreements rather than resolves them. *Know why you are uncomfortable with the other person's anger,* and at a calm time explain your position to him or her.

Second, as you respond to his anger, remember that *anger is not the true emotion.* Regardless of how intense and destructive the other person's anger is, it is still an expression of their fear, hurt, or frustration. Unfortunately, the anger camouflages this and doesn't clearly identify the problem for you. If you can give the person permission in your own heart and mind to be angry, it will be easier for you not to respond in anger yourself. Then you can concentrate on the real issue between the two of you as well as the underlying cause of the anger. When you can learn to avoid responding to another person's anger with your own, you have taken a giant step forward.

There are several ways in which you can help to defuse the anger of another person. One way is for you to heed a "prior agreement." Sometimes parents and children (or couples) work out an agreement or covenant on how they will act during their disagreements. The first step is for you to adhere to the covenant-agreement. Here are two points from an agreement that one couple developed in order to improve their communication and problem-resolving skills:

1. We will not exaggerate or attack the other person during the course of a disagreement.
   a) I will stick with the specific issue.
   b) I will take several seconds to formulate words so that I can be accurate.
   c) I will consider the consequences of what I say before I say it.
   d) I will not use the words always, all the time, everyone, nothing, and so forth.

2. We will attempt to control the emotional level and intensity of arguments. (No yelling, uncontrollable anger, hurtful remarks.)
   a) We will take time-outs for calming down if either of us feels that our own anger is starting to elevate too much. The minimum amount of time for a time-out will be one minute and the maximum ten minutes. The person who needs a greater amount of time in order to calm down will be the one to set the time limit. During the time-out each person,

individually and in writing, will first of all define the problem that is being discussed. This will include, first, identifying the specific cause for anger. Second, the areas of agreement in the problem will be listed. Third, the areas of disagreement will be listed, and fourth, three alternate solutions to this problem will be listed. When we come back together the person who has been the most upset will express to the other individual, "I'm interested in what you've written during our time-out. Will you share yours with me?"

b) Before I say anything I will decide if I would want this same statement said to me with the same words and tone of voice.[26]

Zones of Anger

Some people like to use a stress-reduction card to measure their excitement. A small chemically treated square, sensitive to heat and moisture, measures a person's level of stress. You place your thumb on the square for ten seconds, and your level of stress will turn the square either black, red, green, or blue, depending upon how tense or excited you are. The green or blue color zone reflects calm, with little or no stress.[27]

There are proper zones to stay in with anger as well. Family members often move out of the temperate (green or blue) zone of anger into a red zone. Temperate is being objective and logical. Red is intense, irrational anger. In between, in what is called a yellow zone, the person feels anger toward the other person but is able to exert control over his thoughts and actions. He can still let the other know that he is angry and needs to express it, but not at the expense of the relationship.

When a person moves from the yellow to the red zone, all the symptoms of the yellow zone have been intensified. This "red" anger is characterized by attacking the person rather than the problem, being irrational, hurling accusations, and demeaning the other person's character. You believe the other person deserves everything you're dishing out. This is where lasting damage can occur. The blue zone is characterized by calm presentations and listening.[28]

It is possible to learn to identify which zone you are in, let the other person know, and also identify which zone you are working toward. As one husband said, "I'm hovering between the yellow and red, and I don't like it either. I want to get rid of how I'm feeling and get into the blue zone. Please listen to me."

Some couples make little flags of each color and pin them up in a predesignated spot to denote the level of their anger. (Some have made this a family project in which everyone has his or her own set of flags. Each keeps his set of flags with him during a discussion or disagreement and holds the appropriate one to let other family members know his anger level.) When a person has chosen to use the flags to convey a message about his anger, he does have some control over his emotions.

Talk or Write?

In this process of defusing yourself and the other person, it may be helpful to ask, "What would be best for us right now? To *talk* about our anger or to *write* it out?" For those who have difficulty verbalizing, writing may help them release feelings that they tend to carry inside. And for the highly verbal, writing may keep them from saying too much at the wrong time. In addition, writing often helps us to see the issues more clearly than talking about them. You can decide whether to reveal what you have written or keep it just for your own expression.

When you write, you can simply list your feelings and identify the cause of your anger. You can say what you would never say directly to the other person, or you can write an angry (unmailed) letter, which you might read aloud in an empty room. Then burn or destroy the letter. Once the letter is destroyed, go back to your spouse and discuss the problem.

7

*A*nger and Forgiveness

How can you keep anger from escalating in any relationship? These guidelines can work for you, but you must be willing to implement them regardless of what others do.

1. Don't wait for your feelings to accumulate. Express your hurt, fear, or frustration as soon as you become aware of it.

2. Be sure to share in the language style of your partner. If the other person uses few words (a condenser) in his or her communication style, keep it brief. If he likes to expand and explain (an amplifier), offer details and sufficient information.

3. The longer you wait to express your feelings, the longer it will take to resolve them. Therefore, you decide whether you want a long or a brief discussion. You do have a choice in the matter. Suggest the amount of time.

4. Don't imply or hint that the other person has ulterior motives or isn't trustworthy. He will turn you off if you do.

5. Any attempts to make the other person feel guilty will come back to haunt you. Your purpose is to *resolve*.

6. Choose an attitude that says you *will* resolve the issue and there *will* be a positive result eventually. Be future-oriented.

7. If the other person makes an attacking personal comment, don't invest your time and energy in responding to it. Let it slide and keep on target.

8. If you make a generalization or embellish the facts (you know, lie a bit), stop at once and correct yourself. Use statements such as "I'm sorry, what I really meant to say and what is more factual is . . ." Whenever you realize that your statements are not what is best, correct yourself and admit to what you have done. It's all right to say, "I was wrong in what I said . . . ," "I was trying to get back at you because. . . ," "I admit I was trying to hurt you, and I'm sorry," or "I was upset at something else, and I took it out on you."

9. Don't give ultimatums during your discussion. Even if one is to be given, this is not the best time, and it reflects a control issue or power struggle. Rarely does it work.

10. Now it's up to you to list three other guidelines that you feel would be positive and helpful. If you want this list of guidelines to work, read it aloud every day for three weeks, and you will find yourself changing.[29]

Remember: Your behavior is not dependent upon what others do. If it is, you have chosen to fall under their control.

The wise King Solomon reminds us that controlling our anger makes good sense: "Good sense makes a man restrain his anger, and it is his glory to overlook a transgression or an offense" (Proverbs 19:11 AMP). You may want to write out how you see yourself putting this verse into daily practice.

When you feel strong anger toward your spouse, sit down and write a list of your feelings. Write honestly and passionately—just as you feel. Exclamation points and underlining are allowed. At the end of the list write the reason for your anger. Identify the cause.

If you prefer, write an angry letter to your mate. Again, be honest about your feelings. You may read the letter aloud in an empty room. Then destroy the letter.

Expressing Anger Positively

When you find yourself getting angry at others, consider these ways to express your anger, since these approaches will heal rather than hurt relationships, encourage rather than discourage.

1. *Don't overreact.* Neither minimize nor maximize the situation. Don't assume you know what the problem is. The most important issue isn't what you think of the problem but how the other person perceives the problem. So listen. Then ask questions. If there is more than one person involved, hear all sides of the story. Give others time to explain their perspective. James 1:19 says that we are to be "a ready listener" (AMP).

Anger involves strong feelings that shouldn't be ignored or denied. An angry outburst is not necessarily the sign of a major problem. When parents overreact to their child's anger, the covert message is "Anger is bad. When you get angry you are bad, and you are wrong." Like adults, children have flashes of anger. However, children's anger is unlike adult anger in one very important way: Children do not usually carry grudges, harbor resentment, or plan ways to get revenge. Because of their limited perspective on life and short attention span, most children easily forgive and forget. They tend to take life as it comes and then let it go. Each day is fresh and new to the child.[30] Perhaps children have something to teach us.

2. *Use the first-person singular pronoun* when you confront another person. Clearly identify your own feelings with "I" statements rather than "you" statements. When you begin with "you," your statements will often come across as demeaning, demanding, and accusatory. You're pointing your finger. By making "I" statements, you can make your point with greater clarity and with less probability of damaging another

person's sense of identity. Consider these examples of healthy "I" statements:

> I am very angry right now.
>
> I need to take a time-out to think and pray about what I'm feeling.
>
> It's hard for me to concentrate on my driving when we're upset like this.
>
> I'd like us to take a ten-minute time-out.
>
> I'm exhausted, and I need some peace and quiet now. I will be willing to talk about this afterward.
>
> I'll be glad to help you with it after dinner.
>
> I don't like it when you talk to me like that.
>
> I would appreciate your saying . . .

3. *Stay in the present.* Don't dredge up all the past failures.

4. *Keep it short and simple.* Have you ever been in a situation where a parent, spouse, or boss was correcting you and he or she seemed to go on and on? Do you remember what that felt like? Do you remember what you would have liked to say to the person? Did it increase your motivation to listen? Did it encourage you? Probably not.

All of us have limited attention spans. The people who make television commercials know this, and they structure their expensive messages accordingly. The shorter and simpler your message, the greater the probability that other people will be able to receive it.

5. *Be specific.* Focus on the essential. Make the expression of your anger descriptive, accurate, and to the point—not several points but one point. What's the bottom line? What's negotiable and nonnegotiable? Do you know? Does the other person know?

6. *Ask yourself, "What's my motive?"* What do I want to accomplish? How can I use this situation to communicate my

love and concern, draw us closer together, and strengthen the bonds of trust? Your goal should be to communicate your anger in such a way that the other person knows he or she is still valuable and important.

The Poison of Unresolved Anger

Anger unresolved won't stay the same. It usually builds into resentment, that feeling of ill will toward another person. It is usually accompanied by the desire to make him pay.

Think about this: When you hold resentment for another person, you have given him or her control of your emotional state. How do you feel about that? Most of us want to feel like we are in control of our own emotions. But you are not in control if you resent someone else! You have shifted the power source to that person. You are letting him or her push your emotional buttons of anger, frustration, and bitterness.

The question you must ask yourself is, "Do I want to let go of my resentments or do I want revenge?" Many people struggle with letting the other person off the hook by forgiving him. With one foot on the road to forgiveness and the other on the road to revenge, you are immobilized. Why not make a commitment one way or the other?

If the part of you that wants revenge is stronger than the forgiving part, then how are you going to get revenge? Does the other person know of your resentment? Is he or she aware of your craving for some kind of vengeance? Have you written out your plan of attack, with specific details of what you will do? Have you bluntly told him about your feelings and your plans to get back at him? If not, why not? If revenge is what you want, why not get it over with and free yourself so your life can be full and unrestricted?

Your reaction is probably "That's crazy! What a ridiculous idea! How could you suggest such a thoroughly unbiblical idea! I would never want to do that, and even if I wanted to, I couldn't do it." Really? Then why not choose the other alternative—to give up your resentment completely and be washed clean of your resentful feelings?

Giving up your resentment may also involve giving up having someone else to blame for the predicament you're in, feeling sorry for yourself, and talking negatively about the other person. You're right—forgiveness costs. But the price tag of resentment demands continual payments.

Overcoming Resentment

There are numerous ways to overcome resentment. First, list all the resentments you have regarding the person you are angry and resentful toward. List each hurt or pain you recall in as much detail as possible. Write out exactly what happened and how you felt then and feel now.

One person shared the following list of resentments:

> I feel hurt that you made sarcastic remarks about me in front of others.
>
> I'm angry that you found it hard to ever give me approval.
>
> I resent that you wouldn't listen to me.

Another shared about her resentment toward her father:

> I hate the fact that you called me trash and treated me the same.
>
> I resent the fact that you ran around on my mom and made me carry that secret as well.
>
> I feel offended by the way you try to use me for your own benefit.
>
> I resent you not loving me for who I am.
>
> I feel indignant over the fact that I am messing up my life today because of wanting to prove to you I'm no darn good, just as you said I was.
>
> I resent you and all men.

Be aware that you may experience so⟨...⟩ upheaval as you make your list. Other old, buried ⟨...⟩ surface at this time. You may feel upset for a wh⟨...⟩ and during this writing, ask God to reveal to you t⟨...⟩ memories, so all of the resentments can be emptie⟨...⟩ God that it is all right for you to wade through and exp⟨...⟩ ⟨...⟩ese feelings at this time.

Don't show these lists to anyone else.

Second, after writing as many resentments as possible, stop and rest for a while. By doing this you may be able to recall other resentments you need to share. You will probably not remember every one. You don't need to.

Third, upon completion of the writing, go into a room with two chairs. Imagine the other person sitting there and accepting what you are verbally sharing with him. Take your time, look at the chair as if the person were there, and begin reading your list. At first you may feel awkward, even embarrassed. But these feelings will pass. You may find yourself amplifying what you have written as you share your lists. In time you'll find your feelings of resentment diminishing.

Another helpful method is to write an unmailed letter to the resented person. Be sure that you *do not* actually give this letter to the individual in mind. For some people the written sharing may be more helpful than the verbal.

Start your letter as you would any letter: Dear_____. This is not an exercise in style or neatness or proper punctuation. You are simply identifying, expressing, and draining your feelings. At first it may be difficult, but as you begin you will feel the words and feelings flowing. Let out all the feelings that have been churning underneath. This is not a time to evaluate whether the feelings are good or bad, right or wrong. They are there and need to be drained.

As I work with people in counseling and have them write such a letter, I ask them to bring it to their next session with me. Often they hand me the letter as they enter the room. "No," I say, "I'd like you to keep the letter, and we will use it a little while." At the appropriate time I ask them to read the letter aloud. Since there is an empty chair in the room, I ask them to imagine that the resented person is sitting in the other chair, listening to the reading of this letter.

I remember one person who wrote a very extensive letter and was surprised when I asked her to read it in my presence. During the first 15 minutes of reading this letter to her mother, the client was also crying and tearful. But during the last five minutes, the crying ceased. There was a positive, bright lilt to her voice as she concluded her letter. Through this experience her resentment drained.

Forgiveness Versus Resentment

Do you know what the opposite of resentment is? That's right: *forgiveness*. You may not forget what the person did which angered you so much; you may remember. On the other hand, perhaps forgetting can occur. Consider this:

> Webster's definition of *forget* can give you some insight into the attitude and response you can choose. Forget means "to lose the remembrance of . . . to treat with inattention or disregard . . . to disregard intentionally; overlook; to cease remembering or noticing . . . to fail to become mindful at the proper time."

Not forgiving means inflicting inner torment upon ourselves. Forgiveness is saying, "It's all right, it's over. I no longer resent you or see you as an enemy. I love you even if you cannot love me back."

Lewis Smedes said:

> When you forgive someone for hurting you, you perform spiritual surgery inside your soul; you cut away the wrong that was done to you so that you can see your "enemy" through the magic eyes that can heal your soul. Detach that person from the hurt and let it go, the way children open their hands and let a trapped butterfly go free.

Then invite that person back into your mind, fresh, as if a piece of history between you had been erased, its grip on your memory broken. Reverse the seemingly irreversible flow of pain within you.[31]

We are able to forgive because God has forgiven us. He has given us a beautiful model of forgiveness. Allowing God's forgiveness to permeate our lives and renew us is the first step toward becoming a person of forgiveness.[32] Consider this prayer of forgiveness from an angry person.

Loving God, I praise You for Your wisdom, for Your love, for Your power. Thank You for life, with its joys and mysteries. Thank You for emotions—including anger.

Forgive me when I am led by my anger instead of being led by You. Make me aware of the things I do that produce anger in others—help me change those things. Show me how to clean up the offenses I commit toward others, and give me the courage to ask forgiveness.

Help me to be able to look past the anger of another person and see Your creation in them, and to love them. Teach me how to forgive; and give me the humility to forgive gracefully.

Arouse me to oppose injustice and other evils. Show me how to channel my energy that might otherwise be wasted in anger into constructive action in Your service.

You ask me to minister to persons around me. Help me understand what that means. Wake me up. Help me recognize that every moment of my life is an opportunity for Your love to flow through me.

Thank You, heavenly Father, for Your love. Thank you for sending Christ so that we might have life and have it to the full, and for sending the Holy Spirit to comfort and guide us through the uncertainties and confusion of everyday living.

In Christ's name. Amen.[33]

The Answer to Stress

8

What Is Stress?

The thief comes only to steal and kill and destroy;
I have come that they may have life,
and have it to the full."

—JOHN 10:10.

What is stress exactly? Stress is *any life situation that chronically bothers, irritates, or upsets you.* It is any type of action that places conflicting or heavy demands upon your body. What do these demands do? They simply upset your body's equilibrium.

Our bodies come equipped with a highly sophisticated defense system that helps us cope with those events in life which threaten and challenge us. When any of us feels pressured or threatened, our body quickly mobilizes its defenses for "fight or flight." In the case of stress, we are infused with an abundance of adrenaline, which disrupts our normal functioning and creates a heightened sense of arousal.

We're like a rubber band that is being stretched. Usually, when the pressure is released, the rubber band returns to normal. When it is stretched too much, though, or kept in that position too long, the rubber begins to lose its elasticity, becoming brittle and developing cracks. Eventually it breaks. That is similar to what happens to us if there is too much stress in our lives.

What is stressful to one individual, however, may not be stressful to another. For some people, stress is worry about future events that cannot be avoided, and then concern about the events after they have occurred. For others, stress is simply the wear and tear of life. It has been called an "influential force."

Although some people think of it as tension and some as anxiety, not all stress is bad. We need a certain amount of pressure and stimulation in order to function properly in life. Stress can be good if it is short-lived. It's when stress is *too much* that we end up crippled. And the wrong type of stress wipes out our spiritual joy as well. Good stress is called "*eu*stress," from the Latin word *eu,* meaning good. It is positive and helpful because it does not last, nor is it experienced continually. It can push us to make some positive changes. Good stress is a form of resistance that stretches us, but then our body's equilibrium soon returns to normal. When our body does not return to normal rest and recovery, we have bad stress, or "*dis*tress."

Causes of Stress

The stress in your life can be caused when anything happens that—

- annoys you
- threatens you
- excites you
- scares you
- worries you
- hurries you
- frustrates you
- angers you
- challenges you
- embarrasses you
- reduces or threatens your self-image

Most of the time, however, it is not a particular *event* that causes stress. What then causes the problem? Most situations which produce stress involve some sort of *conflict* between ourselves and the world outside us. For example, if a teen skips school to go to the beach (which fulfills a personal desire), he creates a new problem at school with his absence. If a mother becomes overinvolved at church and then has little time and energy for household responsibilities, there are new demands placed upon her family. If she doesn't balance the demands from outside with those from inside herself, she will experience stress and pressure.

Where does most of our stress come from? Whether we are children, teens, or adults, it comes from *our own minds*. The most damaging stress comes from threats that cannot be acted upon because they exist only in our imagination. Some people imagine the worst in a situation. They worry, which creates more threat and imagined fears. Even when there *is* a definite threat to the body, the basic problem is in the mind. Situations that worry a person can be the most troublesome of all. On the other hand, a person who has learned to live according to "Let not your heart be troubled, neither let it be afraid" (John 14:27 KJV) will be able to handle the pressures of life, both real and imagined, much better.

Stress Symptoms

What about you? Is decision-making becoming more difficult? Even small decisions?

Do you find yourself tending to daydream or to fantasize about "getting away from it all?" Does this happen several times a day? Do you tend to use more medication to settle down? You know—tranquilizers or uppers.

Do you find your thoughts trailing off when you're talking or writing?

What about excessive worrying about all things, including taking on other people's worries as well?

Do you experience sudden outbursts of temper? Is there an increase in the intensity and expression of your anger?

Are you beginning to forget appointments, dates, and deadlines, even though this is not usually your pattern? Is your image of being responsible starting to shatter?

Do you find yourself brooding over events and issues, and not just major ones either? Do little things become the catalyst for sitting and vegetating? Do you increasingly have feelings of inadequacy that have no apparent basis?

Are people beginning to say about you, "You don't seem quite yourself anymore" because they're aware that your typical behavior is changing?

All of the items here are symptoms of stress overload. Do any of them describe you? If so, welcome to the world of stress.

The Three Stress Situations of Life

Stress is a simple, common word. It has been used as a catchall to explain a physical and emotional response when no other explanation can be found. But stress is real.

To become aware of stress in our life, the best way to start is by identifying the three major categories of stress.

The first type of stress is called *Type A* (not to be confused with the "Type A Personality") and is both *foreseeable and avoidable*. If you plan to ride "The Killer" roller-coaster ride or see one of the newest blood-and-gore science-fiction movies, you know in advance the stress you will encounter and are able to avoid it if you so desire.

There is also foreseeable and avoidable stress which is not under your control. The world lives under the threat of running out of natural resources and seeing the environment become more and more polluted. Another threat is the ever-present possibility of nuclear war. Stress from these types of uncertainties is difficult for anyone to handle.

Type B stress situations come from demands which are *neither foreseeable nor avoidable*. These fall into the category of crisis events such as the death of a friend or family member, an accident while in the car or while involved in sports activities, the discovery of your impending divorce or separation, or learning that a sibling is gay or has AIDS.

These stressful situations place the greatest demands upon all of us. Many of these are crises and some could be traumatic.

You must handle your own feelings, the situation itself, and the response of other people as well. Both the person who has to face a divorce and the teen with a torn tendon, which eliminates his chances of a college sports scholarship, have to adjust in two main ways: (1) thinking about themselves with a new perspective, and (2) relating to others in a different fashion.

The third type of stress situation, *Type C*, is *foreseeable but not avoidable*.

The most damaging stress comes from threats that cannot be acted upon because they exist only in our imaginations. Some of us imagine the worst in a situation. We worry, which creates more stress and imagined fears. Even if there is a definite threat to the body, the problem is in our mind. Learning to live according to "Let not your heart be troubled, neither let it be afraid" (John 14:27 KJV) will handle the pressures of life, both real and imagined, in a much better fashion.

Let's consider another way in which our thought life is affected. Dr. Jack Haskins, head of the communications department at the University of Tennessee, conducted a 12-year study on the impact of bad news. Here is what he concluded about the results of a five-minute radio broadcast with four items of bad news:

1. It always leaves you more depressed.
2. It leaves you with a perception of the world and others which is more negative.
3. It leaves you inclined to help others less—why bother?
4. Hearers of bad news overestimate the possibility of being the victims of violence and bad news.

5. About 95 percent of what impacts us in America is negative.

6. There are 50 percent more bad news items in U.S. broadcasts than in Canada.

What is the first thing you listen to on the radio in the morning? What is the last TV program you watch at night before you try to go to sleep?

The Stress of Christian Myths

Some of our stress comes from beliefs that we hold on to even though they are neither accurate nor healthy. Judson Edwards suggested the following myths of uptight Christianity which limit us:

1. God will love me more if I *do* more. (Truth: God loves me completely right now. All of the sweat-soaked piety and goodness I can muster cannot add one jot or tittle to His love.)

2. It is more Christian to work than to play. (Truth: The truest test of our faith is our capacity to laugh, to treasure life, and to celebrate God's goodness.)

3. I can't make any mistakes because the world is watching my witness. (Truth: It is a serious mistake to think I will never make a mistake and a presumptuous mistake to think the world is particularly interested in my life.)

4. I am the only Bible some people will ever read. (Truth: God is at work in the world, and if by some strange, unforeseen chance I should pass from the scene, He will be able to manage without me.)

5. Morality is the heart of the Christian message. (Truth: Grace is the heart of the Christian message.)

6. On my deathbed I will be sorry I didn't accomplish more. (Truth: If I have time at all for regrets, I will be sorry I didn't love more lavishly and enjoy life more fully.)

7. Most Christians (including myself) are lazy and uncommitted. (Truth: Most Christians [including myself] are burned out and disillusioned.)

8. Most Christians (including myself) need to learn the value of hard work and dogged determination. (Truth: Most Christians [including myself] need to learn to relax and experience joy.)

9. It is wrong and self-centered to concentrate on my joy. (Truth: Joy is one of the proofs of the presence of God in my life.)

10. Life is grim business, and I must treat it seriously. (Truth: Life is a holy gift full of exciting possibilities, and I must live in constant gratitude for it.)

I say it again for emphasis: Much of our misery is self-inflicted. That *sounds* like bad news, but that premise actually holds a concealed promise. For if *we* create many of our stresses, that means *we* are in control of them. What we create, in other words, we can *uncreate*. We are not ragdolls at the mercy of demonic pressures over which we have no power. And if we have chosen to live in ways that induce stress, we can also choose to live in ways that can open the wells of inner peace. Our stress, to a great extent, lies in our own hands.

Here's the dividing line: Until we realize that most stress is a choice, we will never know that we can cross over and move toward inner peace. We will quietly curse our fate, pine for a better job, yearn for a more understanding family, and become more and more miserable as the days go by. As long as we think all stress comes from "out there," we will make little effort to deal with it. Why battle the inevitable?[34]

9

ʃtress in Women

We have looked at the characteristics of being stressed. But now let's get specific. What contributes to stress, say, in a woman's life?

What is stressful to one woman may not be to another. Your background, your life experience, how you learned to handle the upsets of life, and your neurological structure will all affect your response to potentially stressful situations.

Remember, not all stress is bad. Good stress can motivate and activate us, and it doesn't last long. It brings a feeling of exhilaration.

One woman therapist searched through a decade of therapy notes with her female clients and looked for the stresses that women could call their own.

- There are the stresses associated with physiology: breast development, menstruation, pregnancy, and menopause.

- There are the stresses connected to life changes: becoming a wife or a mother, enduring a divorce or economic collapse, moving into the forties in a youth-oriented society, having adult children return home, and widowhood.

- There are the psychological stresses experienced by the lonely single woman and the homemaker coping with the pressure to break out of the routine and go back to school or develop a career. There are the stresses experienced by the career woman who is being pressured to give it up, go back home, and be a family member, or the stress endured by an exhausted working woman constantly short on sleep and money.

- There are the not-so-apparent stressors that tend to not only distract a woman but over time deplete her resources, leading to a feeling of distress. Those stressors include the pressure of commuting, being isolated with young children, crime and the threat of being attacked because of being a woman, fighting the chauvinism of others, and sexist comments as well as harassment.

- Finally, there are the life crises that unfortunately tend to be handled more by women than by men. These can include caring for a sick or dying parent or child, parenting a handicapped child, and handling the aftermath of her own or her child's divorce.[35]

Why Women Experience Stress

Let's take a closer look at some of the reasons why any woman today might experience stress.

Barriers, contradictory feelings, changing expectations. In *Beyond Chaos: Stress Relief for the Working Woman*, Sheila West talks about "the glass ceiling" and what West calls "the reeling effect." The glass ceiling is a perceived barrier that allows women to glimpse, but prevents them from obtaining, positions further up the corporate ladder.

The reeling effect is difficult to overcome, since its ingredients are change plus apprehension, equaling uncertainty. Many women experience this phenomenon. Constant change along with apprehension about their work leaves them feeling as though they just stepped out of a tornado.[36] It's the mixture of opposing feelings: "Oh, I really want to work" versus "When am I going to be able to quit?" and "Is it always going to be like this?"; "This is so challenging and informative" versus "How will I survive all these deadlines? Help!" Sheila West comments on the contradictory feelings that create the sense of uncertainty in women:

> For many women, indecisiveness arises when they simply occupy a job slot instead of effectively creating a career path. A job is accepting a task that has to be done. A career is the pursuit of results that have a long-term significance, even if that pursuit is on a short-term basis.

> If I go to work just because I have a job, it confines my perspective to a narrow slice of reality. The phrase "just a job" conjures up unpleasant associations: mundane assignments, boring routines, something to be endured. In this kind of environment, our feelings are bound to fluctuate with daily activities in an aimless moodiness. All too soon we start asking, "What now?" When we're not sure what we're accomplishing or what the ground rules are for doing it, and we receive a meager paycheck to boot, we'll continue to question whether we made the right choice.

> But women who are trapped in entry-level jobs are not the only ones suffering from the clash of expectations and reality. Even women on a career track are often caught off guard with what they find in the marketplace. There doesn't seem to be much security or continuity in many fields.

> Women often find that staying on the competitive edge means treacherous climbing rather than sustaining accomplishments. The thrill of a new challenge gives way to the agony of moving too fast to be adequately prepared. We thought we knew what we wanted, but once we get it we're not sure it's what we had in mind.

> The reeling effect keeps us frustrated over the constant effort to prove ourselves, the energy required to avoid unnecessary confrontations with others, and the enduring

stress of having to maintain high-quality performance. The stress can reach the point where even if we do love work, we want out anyway. The pleasure of accomplishment is just not worth the struggle for survival.[37]

Single in a married world is another problem. Today's woman is more likely to experience a divorce. Estimates are that one-half to two-thirds of women who married in the eighties will end up divorced. More women than before will never marry, and more of those who do won't ever have a child. A greater number of women are less dependent on men. In 1990 only 31 percent of women believed that to be really happy, they needed a man. In 1970, 66 percent believed that.[38]

Nevertheless, if you're single you'll experience stress because of it, especially if you're getting older and want to get married. If you're older than 34 you have a problem, as the pool of eligible men is very small. The stress of "I must find a man" that propels many women in their thirties and forties keeps them from living a full life.

There is another stress as well: How does our society view single women? Is it a positive or a negative view? The stereotype is that single women are unhappy and perhaps defective in some way.[39]

New freedoms, fewer options. What generates much stress and anger is that few women end up having the life they thought they were going to get when they were growing up. Yes, there are new freedoms and changes, but there are also fewer options. A permanent marriage, children, and handling work and home are not sure things. Life is more unpredictable. We used to hear that women could have everything they ever wanted. Many have become disenchanted with that idea: Not only is it not working out, but what accompanies the new options and lifestyle is enormous stress, much more than ever before.

The doors have opened more work for women, but that has added much more stress to women's lives. Working wives and mothers have discovered that they are still expected to run the home and fulfill the same duties they did when they were at home. Husbands do not help out that much, partly because they are let off the hook too easily. Naturally, that causes stress and anger and eventually resentment.

Guilt over working. Many working wives, and especially mothers, struggle with guilt over working. To make up for it, they put forth a double effort at home to show they are adequate mothers and can handle both work and homemaking. Soon they're stressed, running on an empty tank, and candidates for burnout.[40]

Housewife in a troubled marriage. Many times I've heard people say that in the end the most fulfilled women will be the ones who stayed at home ("where they belong" is usually implied) and raised their children. If you're among those who agree with that statement, you may be surprised at the findings of the 1990 report from the American Psychological Association National Task Force on Women and Depression.

The report cites a study that ranked women from least depressed to most depressed, starting with the least depressed. Here is that ranking, with least depressed women listed first:

1. Employed wives with a combination of low marital strain and low job strain.
2. Employed wives with low marital strain but high job strain.
3. Unmarried women with low job strain.
4. Nonemployed wives with low marital strain.
5. Employed unmarried women with high job strain.
6. Employed wives with high marital strain and low job strain.
7. Nonmarried, nonemployed women.
8. Employed wives with high marital strain and high job strain.
9. Nonemployed wives with high marital strain.

The happiest women are those who are pleased with both their jobs and their marriages. The least happy women—they have 5½ times the risk of depression as the first—are housewives with troubled marriages.[41]

Too much to do, too little time. Time is one of the stress-inducers for many women. Even when they have financial problems, two out of three women say they would prefer more time rather than money.[42]

Many women tend to add pressure to their lives by taking on too much or attempting to accomplish too much in a limited time span. Often they continually take on new activities, never evaluating which ones are really important and therefore never dropping any. Time-pressured women may be driven by their own unrealistic ideals, by the expectations of others, or both.

Fatigue. As stated in an earlier chapter, women identified fatigue as the number one contributor for making them vulnerable to anger. Fatigue is also one of the main contributors to depression—and to stress. Many women, single and married, begin to feel worn down as they try to juggle having a career with the other demands in their lives.

Insufficient sleep is also a major factor here. In the book *Losing Sleep* it is suggested that there is an epidemic of sleepiness sweeping the globe.[43] *Time* magazine points to mounting evidence that sleep deprivation has become one of the major problems in our country.[44]

The majority of women do not get the seven to eight hours of sleep a night that sleep experts tell us we need in order to function at our best. They average only five to six hours a night—an insufficient amount, which over time will erode a person's resources. Too little sleep results in less emotional control, less energy, less clear thinking, and a greater tendency to be at risk for illness, accidents, conflict, and anger.[45]

Boredom. Boredom—or lack of meaning in what you do—can cause stress. This may come as a surprise to you, but it's true: continually doing the same routine or being bored can become a stressor. Homemakers and those in routine jobs may struggle with this. Sometimes a woman may have to work at discovering the meaning in what she is involved in doing. She may need to become creative and develop some new ways of responding to a monotonous environment.

Unrealistic expectations. Unrealistic expectations will keep you stressed. We all have expectations for ourselves and for others. But can they all be attained? Where did they come from? Perfectionists are people with excessively unobtainable expectations. They are great candidates for stress. There is a difference between living a life of perfectionism (or attempting to, since no one has ever been successful at it yet) and a life of excellence. The dictionary states that to be perfect is to be "complete and flawless in all respects." Excellence is defined as something "outstandingly good or of exceptional merit." Perfection is defined by absolutes. Excellence, on the other hand, means you do things to the best of your ability, but you still make mistakes.

Perfectionism is an end state, whereas excellence leaves room for growth. Aiming for excellence allows for forgiveness. A perfectionist may be 98 percent successful in something but allows the 2 percent to white out all the success. She focuses on the flaw and doesn't see the value in progress. Remember that if you are striving to be a perfectionist, you are still living by works and have not yet learned to live by the grace of God. If perfectionism is a struggle for you, perhaps you would benefit from reading *Hope for the Perfectionist,* by David Stoop.

Role conflicts. Role conflicts will contribute to stress. If you are in a job ill-suited to you, it may be stressful. If you are a housewife and would rather be following a career, you may experience stress. Feeling stuck will build your anger.

Communication blocks. If you are dating or married and open communication is blocked, stress will build. Relationships are built upon communication. When a spouse or parent refuses to talk or puts pressure on others to be quiet, there will be damaging results. In a marriage relationship, when one partner is either overly quiet or pulls the silent treatment, very little intimacy can develop. This is one of the major causes of marital disruption and destruction.

Pressures of the workplace. The nineties ushered in what is referred to as "the era of the new woman." Many more women work than ever before. It is estimated that 90 percent of the women in this country have worked or will work for pay at some time during their lives. Most women work because they have to, but many have said they would work even if they didn't need to, because they have assessed the benefits of being employed. Many more women today see their work as a career rather than just a job, which means they have a greater personal investment in it.

The jobs that women hold today are more of the stressful, pressure-laden ones. In 1988 women made up 39 percent of all the personnel holding managerial, executive, and administrative positions—a 13 percent jump from ten years before.

Women have discovered that work not only brings in money but can generate stress. Sometimes the stress overrides the benefits. Many factors contribute to that stress:

- Having a great deal of responsibility, but little authority or control.

- Having an abundance of work, but insufficient time to complete it.

- Having a strong desire to advance in your job, but the chances are limited.

- Discovering you are more competent than your boss, but are still being ignored.

- Being underpaid for what you do, or discovering that men in the same position are paid more.

- Having a lot to do, but constantly being interrupted.

- Doing work that is not exciting, challenging, or stimulating, but is instead boring and redundant.

- Experiencing sexual harassment or discrimination on the job.
- Holding a clerical job (where the above factors are experienced most frequently). [46]

The Type A Woman

The "Type A Syndrome," described by cardiologists Meyer Friedman and Ray Rosenman, used to be a condition mostly experienced by achievement-oriented males. But article after article is now discussing this condition as a definite potential for women in high-pressure jobs. The most dangerous factors connected with this problem are time urgency and chronic anger. Much of the anger stems from insufficient time and too much to do, unrealistic expectations, and guilt.

A Type A woman or man experiences *free-floating hostility*, a sense of lasting, indwelling anger. This hostility increases in frequency, demonstrating itself even in the most minor frustrations. A Type A woman may be clever at hiding this tendency or finding excuses and reasons for her irritation. But she becomes upset too frequently, and in ways that are out of proportion to the irritants. She is overly and outwardly critical and belittles and demeans others.

A Type A person's *sense of time urgency* manifests itself in two ways. First, she speeds up her activities. The way she thinks, plans, and carries out tasks is accelerated. She talks faster and forces others to do the same. It is difficult to relax around her. Everything must be done faster, and she looks for ways to increase the speed. Second, she has many different thoughts and activities on the burner at the same time. Leisure time doesn't reduce the tension, for she overschedules activities even then. She attempts to find more time and tries to do two or three things at once. She overextends herself in a multitude of activities and projects, and often some go undone.

In time your body will tell you if your behavior is Type A. A true Type A person's body excretes more adrenaline, a hormone which constricts the blood vessels and pushes up blood pressure.

Cumulative Stress

In the 1970s two medical doctors named T. H. Holmes and R. H. Rahe developed the Holmes-Rahe stress test, which has been widely used and was recently revised and updated for women. The Holmes-Rahe test is based upon a series of life events, with each event receiving a numeric score for its stress potential or value. In the original sample the researchers discovered that individuals with scores of more than 300 points for the past year had an 80 percent chance of experiencing an illness or depression within the next two years, because of the amount of stress they were experiencing. The results showed the correlation between life-change stress and physical and emotional stress.

In the updated survey, 2300 women in 20 states were surveyed to see how they were affected by the same events listed in the original survey. The top ten stressors are listed below, along with their original ranking and new ranking. The numbers in parentheses are the point values for each.

TOP TEN STRESSORS

New Rank	Stressor	Old Rank
1	Death of spouse (99)	1
2	Divorce (91)	2
3	Marriage (85)	7
4	Death of close family member (84)	5
5	Fired at work (83)	8
6	Marital separation (78)	3
7	Pregnancy (78)	12
8	Jail term (72)	4
9	Death of a close friend (68)	17
10	Retirement (68)	10 [47]

Those who participated in the revised survey were given the opportunity to add new stressors to the original list. The list below shows the top 13 items they mentioned, and also indicates what percentage of the respondents mentioned the item. (Keep in mind that the sample was made up of 2300 women.)

NEW STRESSORS

Stressor	Percentage of Sample Mentioning the Item
Parent's illness	59
Husband's stopping work	58
Child's illness	58
Spouse's illness	55
Chemical dependency	31
Remarriage	29
Commuting	27
Crime victimization	26
Depression	23
Raising teens	22
Husband's retirement	22
Infertility	19
Single parenting	18

It is enlightening to note the stress ratings for these and other new items. They are given below.

STRESS RATINGS FOR THE NEW STRESSORS

Stressor	Points
Disabled child	97
Single parenting	96
Remarriage	89
Depression	89
Abortion	89
Child's illness	87
Infertility	87

Spouse's illness	85
Crime victimization	84
Husband's retirement	82
Parenting parents	81
Raising teens	80
Chemical dependency	80
Parent's illness	78
Singlehood	77[48]

The changes in stress patterns are quite apparent. Where do you fit in all of this? Do you agree with the ratings given to these stressors? What are the five major stressors in your life at the present time? What are the effects in your life because of each one?[49]

How to Lessen Stress

What's the answer? How do you lessen the stress in your life? There are several steps to consider. You could try to change your environment, whether it be working conditions, home schedule, travel, or moving. Some things, however, are difficult to change. Relaxation techniques do help. Tranquilizers are sometimes prescribed for stress, but remember that some people become overly dependent on tranquilizers.

Perhaps the best approach, after you have taken all the corrective action possible, is to change your thoughts and perspective on what is taking place in your life. At the heart of most of life's stress is our attitude—our belief system. If you are stuck on the freeway and have an appointment in 20 minutes for which you will now be late, what do you say to yourself? Many people sit there and begin to fuss and make statements such as "I can't be late! Who's holding us up? How dare they? I've got to get out of this lane!" They begin to lean on the horn and glare at others.

I know it's inconvenient to be stuck, to be late, to have a boss pile on work at the last minute, to miss the bus, or to break a nail just before church. But the key factor that moves you from feeling like a victim to becoming an overcomer is taking control of your circumstances by giving yourself permission to be in the situation you're in: to have your plans disrupted, or to be given too much work, or whatever it may be. That will put you back in control, and you'll feel there is some hope.

It works. I've seen it work. And it can work for you. It's learning to put Philippians 4:13 into practice: "I have strength for all things through Christ who empowers me" (AMP). Proverbs 15:15 applies also: "All the days of the desponding and afflicted are made evil [by anxious thoughts and forebodings], but he who has a glad heart has a continual feast [regardless of circumstances]" (AMP).

Here are a number of suggestions for changing your responses and reducing the stress and fatigue in your life. Making these changes may be uncomfortable at first because you are giving up a way of life that is comfortable, though potentially destructive. It may take awhile for you to see a change, and it will certainly take some effort, but it is worth it in order to reduce the stress in your life.

- Each day think about the causes of your time urgency and the reasons you feel stressed. Write down one of the consequences.

- As part of your new program read *When I Relax I Feel Guilty,* by Tim Hansel, in a leisurely fashion.

- Reduce your tendency to think and talk rapidly by making a conscious effort to listen to others. Become "a ready listener" (James 1:19 AMP). Ask questions to encourage others to continue talking. If you have something to say, ask yourself, *Who really wants to hear this? Is this the best time to share it?*

- Begin each day by asking God to help you prioritize those items that need to be done first. Then do only those items you really have time for. If you feel you can accomplish five items during the day, do only four. Write them down and then check them off.

- If you begin to feel pressured about completing your tasks, ask yourself these questions: *Will completing this task matter three to five years from now? Must it be done now? If so, why? Could someone else do it? If not, why not?*

- Try to accomplish only one thing at a time. If you are going to the bathroom, don't brush your teeth at the same time. If you are waiting for someone on the phone, don't attempt to look through the mail or a magazine. Instead, look at a restful picture or do some relaxation exercises. When someone is talking to you, put down your newspaper, magazine, or work and give the person your full attention.

- Make it a point to relax without feeling guilty. Give yourself permission to relax and enjoy yourself. Tell yourself it is all right, because indeed it is.

- Reevaluate your need for recognition. Instead of looking for the approval of others, tell yourself in a realistic way, "I did a good job and I can feel all right about it."

- Begin to look at the Type A behavior of others. Ask yourself, *Do I really like that person's behavior and the way he or she responds to people? Do I want to be that way?*

- If you have a tendency to ask "How much?" and "How many?" and to think in numbers, change the way you evaluate others or situations. Express your feelings in adjectives and not numbers. (This seems to be harder for men).

- Begin to read magazines and books that have nothing to do with your vocation. Go to the library and check out novels or books on different topics. Become adventuresome, but don't see how many different books you can read, or brag to others about this "accomplishment."

• Play some soft background music at home or at the office to give a soothing atmosphere.

• Attempt to plan your schedule so that you drive or commute when traffic is light. Drive in the slow lane of the highway or freeway. Try to reduce your tendency to drive faster than others or just as fast.

• Pick days to leave your watch at home. Keep track of how often you find yourself looking at your wrist that day.

• Tape-record one of your own phone or dinner conversations and play it back. Note whether you talk most, ask questions, or listen to answers. Do you look for something else to do while you're on the phone? Do you try to speed up your conversation by supplying the endings of sentences for your partner? Do you interrupt or change the topic to fit your needs?

• Don't evaluate your life in terms of how much you have accomplished or how many material things you have acquired. Recall your past enjoyable experiences for a few minutes each day. Take time to daydream about pleasurable experiences as a child.

• Make your noon hour a rest time away from work. Go shopping, browse through stores, read, or have lunch with a friend. After a meal with a friend, make notes about the concerns that person shared with you. Use your notes as a prayer guide. Follow up later to see how the person is doing. You may want to call a different person each week. Let them know you have been praying for them and want to know how they are doing.

• Begin your day 15 minutes early and do something you enjoy. If you tend to skip breakfast or eat standing up, sit down and take your time eating. Look around the house or outside and fix your interest upon something pleasant you have been overlooking, such as flowers in bloom or a beautiful painting.

• Begin to recognize what your values are. Where did they come from, and how do they fit into the teaching of Scripture?

• When you arrive home, announce to others (even if it's just the cat) that the first ten minutes belong to you. When you come home from the office, de-stress yourself before you deal with home. Or read while you have a beverage in a restaurant for ten minutes. Stop at church for five minutes for prayer in the quiet of the sanctuary. Make this a regular part of your day.

• This one will sound crazy, but get in the longest supermarket line to practice waiting without getting upset. Give yourself permission to be in a long line. Discover how you can make time pass pleasantly. Speculate upon the lives of those around you. Talk to them about positive things, not about how long the line is. Review pleasant memories.

• As you play games or engage in sports, whether it be racquetball, skiing, or cards, do it for enjoyment and not for competition. Begin to look for the enjoyment of a good run or an outstanding rally, and the good feelings that come with recreation that you have been overlooking.

• If you have a tendency to worry, begin to follow the suggestions in this book.

• Allow yourself more time than you need for your work. Schedule ahead of time and for longer intervals. If you usually take a half-hour for a task, allow 45 minutes. You will see an increase in the quality of your work.

• Evaluate what you do and why you do it. Lloyd John Ogilvie offers some insights on our motivations and the pressures we create:

> We say, "Look, God, how busy I am!" We equate exhaustion with an effective, full life. Having uncertain purposes, we redouble our efforts in an identity crisis of meaning. We tack up performance statistics in the hope that we are counting for something in our generation. But for what or for whom?
>
> Many of us become frustrated and beg for time to just be, but do our decisions about our involvements affirm that plea? A Christian is free to stop running away from life in overinvolvement.[50]

In one of Dr. Ogilvie's sermons he raised two interesting questions that relate to what we are doing and how we are doing it: "What are you doing with your life that you couldn't do without the power of God?" and "Are you living life out of your own adequacy or out of the abundance of the riches of Christ?" Both questions deserve an honest answer.

The Ultimate Answer to Stress

The real answer to stress is found in applying God's Word to your life. What I have done with many counselees is to suggest that they read the following passages out loud several times a day. You may want to do the same.

> Now to him who is able to establish you in the faith which is in accordance with my Gospel and the preaching of . . . Jesus Christ . . . according to the revelation...of the mystery . . . which was kept . . . secret for long ages (Romans 16:25 AMP).

> Then [Ezra] told them, Go your way, eat the fat, drink the sweet drink, and send portions to him for whom nothing is prepared; for this day is holy to our Lord. And be not grieved and depressed, for the joy of the Lord is your strength and stronghold (Nehemiah 8:10 AMP).

He shall be the stability of your times, a wealth of salvation, wisdom, and knowledge; the fear of the LORD is his treasure (Isaiah 33:6 NASB).

You will guard him and keep him in perfect and constant peace whose mind [both its inclination and its character] is stayed on You, because he commits himself to You, leans on You, and hopes confidently in You (Isaiah 26:3 AMP).

Do not fret or have any anxiety about anything, but in every circumstance and in everything, by prayer and petition [definite requests], with thanksgiving, continue to make your wants known to God (Philippians 4:6 AMP).

Fret not yourself because of evildoers, neither be envious against those who work unrighteousness (that which is not upright or in right standing with God) (Psalm 37:1 AMP).

ʃtress in Men

Stress seems to have more deadly effects on men than on women.

Twice as many men die from combined diseases of the heart as do women.

Pneumonia and influenza cause about three times as many male deaths as female.

Accidents and adverse drug effects kill three times more males than females.

Men commit suicide at a rate of three to one compared to women. There are 30 percent more male deaths than female from cancer (which can be stress related).

Men seem susceptible to stress in other ways as well. More males die as fetuses during their mother's pregnancies, at birth, and as very young babies. Men live shorter lives than women. It appears that from birth to old age, males are more prone to dying before their time than females. And men exhibit more stress-related problems than women, such as hypertension, arteriosclerosis, heart attack, and heart failure.

Life is full of the potential for stress. We all face it. With the increase of information concerning stress during the past decade, a person would have to be blind not to be aware of its existence. Sources of stress cannot always be eliminated, and so the change must come in our *response* to these sources. Men are aware that stress affects their bodies and their behavior, but they need to be convinced that the damage is happening *now!*

I have talked to many men who say they know that in time stress will have a negative effect on their life, but they emphasize "in time." A hint of denial exists. Many men have to feel the symptoms first before admitting there is a problem. As one 40-year-old man said, "Look, I haven't had any heart problems, or ulcers or high blood pressure. I'm really all right. When my body begins to cry out to me, then I'll listen." The problem with this approach is that changes occur slowly and quietly. A man's body may be crying out with a silent scream, but his ears do not hear it. Today's stress is the cause of tomorrow's personal difficulties. Today's stress, unfortunately, affects other people *today*, not tomorrow!

Who takes the brunt of the stress in a man's life? Everyone—his family, his friends, and mainly himself, but especially his heart! The heart is the main target of destruction for much of the harmful stress that a person experiences.

Most people today live in both a competitive and demanding situation. For many men, this starts at a very early age and keeps them striving to get ahead. Many live their lives in a constant state of hurry—even emergency. When this occurs, unconsciously men become dependent upon an overproduction of adrenaline to accomplish their goals. This strategy works, but the cost is much higher than they imagine. The cardiovascular system experiences more and more wear and tear, and most men don't even realize what is happening to them until clear symptoms emerge. You have undoubtedly seen the person who has tolerance for frustration and is highly driven and always in a hurry. Label that person a candidate for heart disease. He (or she) is at high risk for heart attack.

The Four Areas of Stress

Do you know the four major areas of male stress? Georgia Witkin-Lanoil, from her decade of working with men under stress, has clearly identified four major focus areas.

Body concerns. You wouldn't know it to look at some men, but for the majority, their body image *is extremely* important. As boys, height, weight, and athletic ability were primary. As young men, sexual ability was important. In middle age, stamina is a major concern. After that, health becomes the major issue. Men are strong, but which sex lives longer? Men are aware of that discrepancy.

Career concerns. Listen to the question put to a little boy: "What do you want to be when you grow up?" The question is repeated again and again as he grows. Notice that the question is *what.* It isn't *who* he wants to be or *how* he wants to be but *what!* At an early age a man can become preoccupied with his occupation. His identity and self-worth are all wrapped up in the same package. The messages he receives from earliest days are: provide, produce, do well, earn lots of money, make choices, and above all be in control. But life doesn't always turn out as we expect or predict. When his career and work are unpredictable, a man's achievement is stifled, his expectations are unrealistic, and his control is out of reach. The result? Stress grows.

Family Concerns. A man has to adjust to the shift from being a son for 20 years to the role of husband and then father. And the majority of men jump into these roles with little anticipation or preparation. Most men spend more time preparing to get their driver's license than they do in getting married or becoming a father. Men in their twenties assume many roles with many demands, and each role carries the "unpredictable" label. For those who experience divorce and then remarriage, the stresses are multiplied even more.

Personal concerns. Most men do not realize how common personal concerns are. Why? Because too few men share these concerns as well as their inner feelings. Men tend to increase and escalate the intensity of their pressure points. They do this in two major ways—by not sharing their innermost feelings and by lack of close male friends. They go it alone and show the world "I am a man." It appears that setting a good example of strength is more important than resolving inner concerns. But having a confidant is actually better than relying upon inner self-confidence. A lack of communication demonstrating a strong bond with another person is a vital factor in the increase of stress and its effects.

Men and women have many similar stresses, but they also experience many pressures that are dissimilar. And among those they have in common, still there are many differences. Unfortunately, both sexes have little understanding of each other's particular stresses. Men often view women as "complainers." And many women see men's upsets as minimal in comparison to premenstrual symptoms, pregnancy, childbirth, and menopause. Women do have a physical makeup in the reproductive system which both creates stress and is vulnerable to it. But men have a higher *fatality* risk from their stress symptoms. The basic question is not who has it worse, but how can I understand the other person to make it better?

How Men and Women Cope

Let's consider some differences between the coping mechanisms of men and women.

The passage of time with its uncertainties and low factor of predictability can be stressful for both men and women. Men feel their achievement clock is moving too slow. By a certain age they would like to have achieved specific salaries, positions, and types of recognition. Men's decade birthdays are important measures of success. What have you achieved by the time you are 50? Men tend to have bigger celebrations on their fortieth and fiftieth birthdays than do women. In some ways they enjoy drawing attention to these dates.

Both men and women have a *desire to achieve*. But the stress encountered along the way varies for each. Men are taught to be more openly competitive. Whatever you do, "win, win, win." Whether in a group, a team, or an individual activity, *winning* is the best. Men do believe that hard work pays off, but it also creates compulsive competitors. A man competes with others on the job, for a promotion, with the memory of his father—and even with himself!

What are the sources of stress for men? Where there is low job satisfaction, shame and guilt arise. And the more they dislike their work, the more stress men feel when they mention to others what they do for a living. For them work becomes a trap. One of the major stressors today is "downsizing." We live with the fear of companies merging or cutting back. Many men in their early fifties have lost jobs and find that they are no longer marketable in the workforce.

Men seem to increase their symptom list as they age. Note the following chart based upon a survey of men.

Symptoms	*Ages*			
	18–29	30–39	40–49	50+
High blood pressure				X
Muscle aches			X	X
Gastritis/ulcers			X	X
Heartburn		X	X	X
Headache	X	X	X	X

Heart attack! The very mention of it strikes a note of fear into the hearts of most men. Why? Because it is so common, and because men are more prone to die of a heart attack than are women. A man's susceptibility is due not just to his physiology but also to his psychology. The highly achievement-oriented, competitive man who has success in his career is also very prone to experience a heart attack.

Remember that both men and women can be Type A. In addition to the free-floating hostility and sense of time urgency that we discussed earlier, this Type A individual deeply affects the lives of others in a stressful way. His stress feeds the stress of others. Type A behavior is a continuous struggle to achieve more and more, or to participate in more and more activities in less and less time. The Type A man charges ahead, often in the face of either real or imagined opposition from others. He is dominated by an inner hidden insecurity about his status and self-esteem, or he is dominated by superaggressiveness, or both. It is easy for him to be over-bearing and dominating.

The Type A man is competitive. There is nothing wrong with a balanced sense of competition, but the Type A person is out of balance. His sense of competition is intense. Motivation comes from the thrill of victory, and he hates defeat. He competes at work, at play, in the family, and of course with himself. It is difficult to relax around this man.

Impatience is a common characteristic of his. Any delays or interruptions create irritation. But it's all right for him to interrupt other people to show them better and faster ways of doing things. He finishes sentences for people, and even though he knows better, he punches the elevator button several times to speed it up. He has refined numerous ways to glance at his watch or a clock to note the time.

Overscheduling of activities for himself is common, and he will attempt to do the same to others. He has polyphasic behavior and thinking, which means he attempts to do several things at the same time. You can see him drinking coffee, looking at a magazine, talking on the telephone, and beckoning to another person to come into his office. Extreme demands are placed upon his thinking ability, energy source, and even digestion. He feels the only way to get ahead is to function in this way. Why waste time?

Other characteristics include a low tolerance for frustration and a high level of aggression. He cannot relax without feeling guilty, and he often suffers from a low self-image, which leads to the free-floating hostility discussed earlier.

There is a major penalty for choosing to live life in this way. What is it? *The Type A man is five times more likely to have a heart attack than the Type B person.* The Type A person is responsible for wrecked lives and careers for himself and others. There are three arterial diseases believed to be initiated or provoked by Type A behavior: migraines, high blood pressure, and coronary heart disease.

How many of these Type A creatures are there? Depending upon the studies you read and whether the population is urban or rural, it is estimated that between 50 and 70 percent of our population fall into the Type A category to some degree.

Can life in the fast lane be slowed down? Yes! I have seen both men and women change. What can you do to help the man in your life who may be this way? Read! There are suggestions to follow. Start with *Adrenaline and Stress*, by Archibald Hart (Word), and *Treating Type A Behavior and Your Heart*, by Meyer Friedman and Diane Ulmer (Knopf).

How to Recognize Stress

Of all the indicators of stress, behavioral signs are the most helpful because you can recognize them and they are usually repetitive. The following is the result of a Male Stress Survey conducted among hundreds of women. These are the early behavioral signs of stress in men as observed by women.

1. A man becomes verbally abusive or critical of his wife or children. This was reported as number one.

2. Withdrawing and appearing silent or preoccupied was the second-most-frequently reported indicator of stress.

3. Men often tend to overeat and gain weight during times of stress.

4. They also tend to drink more alcohol during stress periods.

5. Unusual fatigue is a stress signal for some men.

6. Some men work off their stress by plunging even more deeply into their work or activities. They exhibit agitated activity.

7. For those who smoke, the smoking rate increases because it is used as an antidote to stress. And during stress it is especially difficult for people to cut back on smoking.

8. Some men experience physical symptoms such as teeth-grinding, tapping the fingers, swinging the feet, or engaging in minor compulsive behaviors when faced with stresses of all types.

9. There is an excessive tendency to fall asleep when faced with stress of all types.

10. Selective deafness is quite common. The man tunes you out even though you think he hears you.

11. Reckless driving and the tendency to take chances reflect stress. The driving pattern can create stress for the other family members as well.

12. Television addiction can be used as a distractor. The man may not even watch the television while it is on; it is just a distractor.

13. Watch for facial gestures such as tics, eyes blinking, excessive swallowing, and so on.

Some of the other characteristics which may occur are increased spending, compulsive sex, or (more commonly) a loss of sexual interest.

What did you notice about the previous list? Did you see how many of these are actually stress distractors and how many can lead to additional stresses? None of these behaviors should be ignored, for they affect the body, the job, and the family.

Early Warning Signs

There are several psychological indicators of stress. Some of these may be characteristics of a man for other reasons, but they are frequently accurate signs that need to be heeded. Any one of these six "D's," as one author has described them, can indicate the beginning of stress. More than one could indicate moderate-to-high stress. I have seen some men with all six warning signs!

Defensiveness is a way of denying that anything is wrong. It can be a way of trying to fool others, or the man can actually believe his own rationalizations. This often reflects the unrealistic expectation that a man should always act like a man: "Be strong and don't admit problems."

Depression is a reflection of loss and anger. And it is the loss of control which bothers so many men.

Disorganization has an effect upon concentration, and thus a man may forget, repeat himself, or not make good decisions. (This is one of the key signs for myself that I am encountering stress. I tend to forget and become a bit disorganized even though I have my two calendars and keep my lists!)

Defiance is a form of attempting to regain control. It gives a man a chance to fight back, even though there is often no real reason for responding in this manner.

Dependency reflects regression, which happens to men under stress. It would be nice to be taken care of, but most men are not about to admit this to someone else.

Decision-making difficulties are common. Even minor decisions may be difficult to make at this time. Feelings of lack of control or choice can block a man from being decisive.

Remember that men differ from each other both in how much stress they can handle and in how they respond to stress. Their tolerance levels vary, and each man experiences stress with a different intensity. Some of a man's symptoms have been learned from role models and from his experiences as he was growing up.

There are many stress-reduction techniques recommended in several books (for example, see *Stress/Unstress: Treating Type A Behavior and Your Heart* and *When I Relax I Feel Guilty,* by Tim Hansel). These include exercise, meditation, relaxation techniques, evaluation of life's goals, and time management. A man needs to become involved in developing healthy responses to the imposed stresses of life and to dis-cover how he creates his own inner stress.

Good Stress/Bad Stress

There are four factors which distinguish between good and bad stress. One is your *sense of choice*. If you *choose* some-thing which carries a sense of pressure, it can feel more like a stimulating experience than stress. Some men have an adren-aline addiction. They thrive on the stimulation of a chal-lenge. They choose the pressure. Unfortunately, there are some who choose too much pressure, and the stimulation becomes excessive and stressful without them knowing what is happening to them.

But when we have pressure put upon us with no control, we experience it as stress.

Second, *control* is a major factor. Real and perceived stress increases as one feels his amount of control diminishing. There are major and minor events which occur in life over which we have absolutely no control. And some of these events come swooping into one's life like an alien invader. Men who have an excessive need for control experience greater stress when they do not have control. In many cases the proportion of control needed by a man is in direct relation to the amount of insecurity hidden behind that controlling veneer.

I'm not sure that we are totally aware of all the sources of stress in our lives. How a man responds to stress will vary from man to man. Some men have learned to accept the unpre-dictability of life and are therefore much better able to handle life's surprises. Others are thrown by life itself. Some men become stressed by changes in simple routines, by going into new social situations, by the fear of failure, and even by their children.

One of the biggest sources of stress occurs when a man feels that a situation is beyond his control. And it can be a very simple situation!

- Men are stressed when they are forced to be in the passenger seat rather than at the wheel of an automobile.

- Men are stressed when they must wait for a table at a restaurant, or in line for a movie, and they frequently choose to forgo the meal or movie to regain their sense of choice.

- Men become infuriated by road construction and exasperated at "stupid" drivers who distract or detain them.

- Men dread funerals and psychotherapy, and sometimes equate the two as depressing reminders of life's uncertainties.

- Men postpone dental appointments and other procedures that require them to put themselves in other people's hands.

- Men are terrified of illness or injury that may interfere with their ability to be in charge of their daily lives.

- Men prefer requests to demands, and free choice to requests, and they will demonstrate this by saying no to suggestions for things that they might actually have enjoyed.

A third stress-related factor is the *ability to anticipate the sequences*. When demands and outcomes are unpredictable, it is more difficult for some men to make the necessary adjustments in life which are predictable. These individuals are bored and stagnating. Others live on the edge of unexpected anticipation constantly and their bodies are wired.

The fourth factor which helps to bring stability and lessen stress even when the first three are lacking is a *person's attitude*—an attitude which has captured the stability of a biblical perspective on life's difficult situations.

Each person has the ability and the freedom to choose his response to life's difficulties and problems. We could say,

"This isn't what I wanted or expected, but here it is and I have to face it. It's going to be a difficult time, but how can I make the best of it and learn through this? How can I grow through this? How can God be glorified through this?"

11

Overcoming Burnout

Today we hear much about a phenomenon called "burnout." How do stress and burnout relate to each other? More and more literature is being written each year to attempt to explain the causes and characteristics of burnout. It appears that during the past 20 years we have developed a new vocabulary in order to explain what is happening to mankind—words such as stress, midlife crisis, and burnout.

Here is a simple overall definition of burnout: "To wear oneself out by excessively striving to reach some unrealistic expectation imposed by oneself or by the values of society."

Another definition is: A burnout is "someone in a state of fatigue or frustration brought about by devotion to a cause, way of life, or relationship that failed to produce the expected reward." Stated another way:

> Whenever the expectation level is dramatically opposed to reality and the person persists in trying to reach that expectation, trouble is on the way.

Burnout has also been defined as a "syndrome of emotional exhaustion, depersonalization, and reduced personal accomplishment that can occur among individuals who do 'people work' of some kind."

Burnout is a response to the chronic emotional strain of dealing extensively with other human beings. If these human beings are troubled, then burnout can be particularly rapid and devastating, and it certainly creates stress!

If you want a simple explanation of how people respond in a burnout, just analyze the word itself. The word "burn" brings about the vision of heat, fire, conflagration, or anger. Some people become angry at their jobs, their families, their friends, or their employers. This is an anger which is seething beneath the surface, ready to boil up and spill over at the slightest provocation.

The second part of the word is "out." There is nothing left. It is as though the person has checked out of life itself. He gives up, claiming that nothing can be done and that the entire mess is hopeless. He hurts others by doing nothing. His energy, integrity, care, love, and desire are gone. Burnout is running on empty.

Five Areas of Burnout

Burnout is a complex process which involves all five major areas of our life: physical, intellectual, emotional, social, and spiritual.

The *physical* aspect refers to the amount of energy available to do what one needs to do and wants to do. Burnout's first symptom is an all-around feeling of fatigue. Usually people suffering from burnout are not involved in exercising or in a nutrition or stress-reduction program.

The *intellectual* aspect refers to the sharpness with which a person thinks and solves problems. In burnout, this ability diminishes. Creativity diminishes, cynicism concerning new approaches increases, and there is no hobby or means of intellectual relaxation.

The *emotional* aspect refers to whether a person's emotional life is basically positive or negative. Is he optimistic or pessimistic about what is occurring in his life? Are there emotional outlets available other than work? Is he aware of what is happening to him emotionally? If he is overinvested in work, and his work begins to deteriorate, his whole life can begin to go downhill. Depression can set in because of the loss of dreams and expectations which have been tied into his work. People with a balanced life of outside interests have a buffer against burnout.

The *social* aspect of burnout refers to feelings of isolation compared to feelings of involvement. What kind of support system does the person have? Does he feel free to share his feelings of frustration, anger, fatigue, or disillusionment? Does he have anyone who will listen? Unfortunately, when a person is experiencing burnout, he often does not want to burden anyone else with his problems, thus creating further isolation for himself.

The *spiritual* aspect refers to the degree of meaning that a person has in his or her life. If his expectations about work have been dashed, he begins to feel a void in his life. His dream about life and his expectations about what God was supposed to do for him become a source of disappointment.

Some burnout can be simply physical. A person may be tired of his job—of the hours or of the ineffectiveness of the system. Usually he recovers after a short vacation or just a day off. Any type of change which brings about a new interest or even a variation of his work routine may help.

Psychological Burnout

The major symptom of burnout is the most serious, and it can happen to Christians and non-Christians alike. It is the deterioration of long-term psychological functioning, which includes the intellectual, emotional, social, and spiritual aspects. There is a decline in happiness, empathy, sensitivity, and compassion. Psychological burnout occurs gradually and is most noticeable when a crisis occurs. The relationships in all areas of life are affected. Recreation becomes mechanical. The person is aloof and distant with friends. He holds his emotions inside and is insensitive to family members.

Psychological burnout takes time to develop and time to reverse. Days off, vacations, or a one-day seminar on stress and burnout are not enough. *Time* plus a reorientation to life are needed. A spiritual renewal through the Word, prayer, and close Christian friendships will also be part of the cure. Part of the reversal also involves looking at the work environment to see if it has contributed to the deterioration.

However, the real problem isn't circumstances as such, but our *response* to circumstances. The Word of God clearly tells us that we will not be free of problems just because our circumstances are calm and peaceful. The experience of peace is a learned response from the application of God's Word in the midst of difficulty.

Burnout Versus Stress

Now let's consider the explicit differences between burnout and stress. Dr. Archibald Hart has suggested the following differences:

- Burnout is a defense characterized by disengagement.
- Stress is characterized by overengagement.
- In burnout the emotions become blunted.
- In stress the emotions become overreactive.
- In burnout the emotional damage is primary.
- In stress the physical damage is primary.
- The exhaustion of burnout affects motivation and drive.
- The exhaustion of stress affects physical energy.
- Burnout produces demoralization.
- Stress produces disintegration.
- Burnout can best be understood as a loss of ideals and hope.
- Stress can best be understood as a loss of fuel and energy.
- The depression of burnout is caused by the grief engendered by the loss of ideals and hope.

- The depression of stress is produced by the body's need to protect itself and conserve energy.
- Burnout produces a sense of helplessness and hopelessness.

Causes of Burnout

What causes burnout? Is it a disease with germs carried about by the winds of life? Where does it originate?

There are numerous causes, but two of the major ones are *expectations* and *distribution*. Unrealistic expectations about life, people, or an occupation can lead to burnout. Some individuals focus upon the goal that they wish to accomplish, with no regard to the struggle involved in the attainment process.

Many people are unaware of the realities of a particular occupation with its pains and struggles. Their dreams of changing the world can be shattered easily. When they realize that they will not be able to change the system, idealism turns to cynicism.

Another facet of unrealistic expectations is the belief that "it can't happen to me." Other people collapse, but not me. Other people fail, but not me. Other people burn out, but not me.

The second major contributor to burnout is *distribution*. You give and give and give, but never receive any replenishment. Soon you're empty.

Overcoming Burnout

What can you do to overcome burnout?

1. Evaluate your goals: What are they and what is their purpose?
2. Evaluate your expectations. List them and discover which ones are realistic and which ones are not.
3. Identify times of stress.
4. Be willing to run the risk of becoming close to others. Let others help carry the responsibility.
5. Learn at least one relaxation technique and practice it on a regular basis. This helps to rest critical components of your body's emergency system.

6. Balance your life by exercising regularly. Good physical conditioning strengthens the body's immune system and increases endorphins, which are the brain's natural tranquilizers.

7. Get proper rest. Allow adequate time for sleep. Contrary to what we have been taught in a previous generation, most of us need more sleep than we get. Adrenal arousal temporarily reduces our need for sleep, but this is a trap because we will ultimately pay the penalty for it.

8. Learn to be flexible. Only the gospel is unchanging. Your ideas and priorities may need to change. Flexibility reduces the likelihood of frustration.

9. Slow down. Remember, God is never in a hurry. "Hurryness" is a human characteristic caused by inadequate planning and poor time management. Hurry speeds up the wear and tear of our bodies and minds and increases the production of destructive adrenaline.

TIME

I wasted an hour one morning beside a mountain stream;

I seized a cloud from the sky above and fashioned myself a dream.

In the hush of the early twilight, far from the haunts of men,

I wasted a summer evening, and fashioned my dream again.

Wasted: Perhaps. Folks say so who never have walked with God,

When lanes are purple with lilacs or yellow with goldenrod.

But I have found strength for my labors in that one short evening hour.

I have found joy and contentment; I have found
peace and power.
My dreaming has left me a treasure, a hope that is
strong and true:
From wasted hours I have built my life and found my
faith anew.
—AUTHOR UNKNOWN

10. Learn constructive ways of dealing with your anger. Our
gospel is a gospel of forgiveness; dispense it liberally to
all who hurt you. Remember that anger is a signal telling
you that something is wrong with your environment, or it
is evidence that you are in "fight-or-flight" mode. Identify
the source of your anger and confront it assertively.

11. Pay attention to the "little hassles," for they are more likely
to kill you than the big ones. It is the everyday, minor irri-
tations that are the deadliest. Keep them to a minimum.

12. Develop your ability to be empathetic in your care of others, and keep your sympathy under control.

13. Focus your work and use of time essentials. Reduce redun-
dancies, eliminate unnecessary activities, avoid demands
that will stretch you too thinly, and learn how to say no
kindly, without giving offense and without experiencing a
sense of guilt.

14. Stay in touch with reality. Don't let your ambitions outrun
the limits of your capabilities. Seek honest feedback from
trusted friends on your talents, then pray for wisdom and
set your sights accordingly. Aiming too high at unrealistic
goals to satisfy an unsanctified ambition will only lead to
burnout.

15. Avoid states of helplessness by taking control and imple-
menting a coping strategy, no matter how minor.
Helplessness is often an erroneous belief that you are
trapped and no solutions are possible. Exercise faith,

believe that solutions are possible, and you can break out of the helplessness cycle.

16. If you cannot resolve a major conflict area in your life, leave it. Move on if necessary. Notions of being superhuman often keep us in severe conflict situations. We believe we should be able to master every circumstance, and this can lead to a persistence that is destructive. Even Jesus was hindered in what He could do (Matthew 13:58) and had to move on. Why not you?

Finally, don't be afraid to seek professional help when you need it.[51]

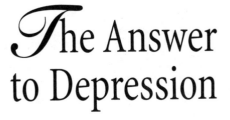

The Answer to Depression

12

Depression: The Unwanted Companion

"I try to do what I need to be doing, but I'm immobilized. The days are gloomy, no matter how bright. The nights seem endless. Apathy blankets me like a shroud. I eat because I have to, but there is no appetite or taste. I feel as though a massive weight is on my shoulders, and fatigue is my constant companion. I pray, I shop, I plead to lift the gloom, but it remains. I've withdrawn from everyone—from family, friends, and even God. Who would want to be around me? I know I wouldn't."

This is the painful cry of a person in the throes of a gripping depression. For some people it's an occasional heavy bout, while for others it's a low-grade depression that seems to be a constant companion. The message of depression is: "You're defeated; there's nothing you can do. There's no way out. It's hopeless."

What Depression Is Like

You probably already know what it's like to be depressed.

It's that feeling of overall gloom—hopelessness, despair, sadness, apathy. A move toward depression is a move toward deadness, and hopelessness is the prevailing feeling. But depression is not like a sense of sadness in which there is a "down" feeling from a disappointment or loss. In a short while

139

this latter feeling lifts, and even when it's your companion you still function well. Depression is different: It lasts longer and is more intense. It can linger and linger with its immobilizing intensity, causing you to lose perspective and making you less able to carry on your life activities. Depression slams down the window of hope, and sometimes it even draws down a darkened shade.

If you think of the literal meaning of the word "depression," it means to move something from a higher position to a lower level. Frequently a depressed person, when asked how he is feeling, will say "quite low."

The loss of perspective that accompanies depression colors the way you experience your life, your tasks, and your family. As one person said:

> There's a real difference between being unhappy and being depressed. When my wife and I have an occasional argument, I'm unhappy about it. I don't like it, but it's part of living. We make up in a fairly short time. I may be concerned over it, but I can sleep all right and I still feel in good spirits. But when I'm depressed, that's a different matter. It hurts all over; it's almost something physical. I can't go to sleep at night, and I can't sleep through the night. Even though there are still times when I'm in pretty good spirits, the mood comes over me nearly every day. It colors the way I look at everything. If my wife and I have a fight, our marriage seems hopeless. If I have a problem at work which I would normally deal with promptly and appropriately, I feel as though I'm a poor teacher. I battle with the problems of self-confidence instead of dealing with the issues in front of me.

When you're depressed you experience changes in physical activities—eating, sleeping, sex. If a lessening of sexual interest occurs, depression may be the cause. Some people lose interest in food, while others gorge themselves. Some sleep constantly; others can't sleep at all. Whatever the particular effects, depression interferes with your ability to function. And if you can function at only 70 percent of your capacity, what does that do? It creates even more depression.

Your self-image tends to plummet. You feel less and less confident about yourself and you question yourself as a person. You withdraw from others because of a fear of being rejected. Unfortunately, when you're depressed your behavior does bring on some rejection from others. You cancel favorite activities, fail to return phone calls, and seek ways to avoid talking with or seeing others. Not only do you want to avoid people, but you also desire to escape from problems, and even from life itself. Thoughts of leaving home or running away, suicidal thoughts and wishes—all these arise because of your feeling that life is hopeless and worthless.

You brood about the past (Psalm 42:4), you become overly introspective, and you are preoccupied with recurring negative thoughts. Your mind replays the same images again and again. You fixate on all the real and perceived wrong things you've done in your life.

When depressed, you're oversensitive to what others say and do. You may misinterpret actions and comments in a negative way. These mistaken perceptions can make you irritable and cause you to cry easily. You exaggerate your own condition. Jeremiah the prophet said, "Desperate is my wound. My grief is great. My sickness is incurable, but I must bear it" (Jeremiah 10:19 TLB).

You have difficulty handling most of your feelings, especially anger. Often this anger is directed outward, against others. But it can also be directed toward yourself: You feel worthless and don't know how to deal with the situation.

Guilt is usually present at a time of depression. The basis for it may be real or imagined. Frequently, guilt feelings arise because you assume you're in the wrong or that your depression is responsible for making other people miserable.

And often depression leads to a state of dependence upon other people. This reinforces your feelings of helplessness; then you may become angry at your sense of helplessness.

Distorting Reality

Depression distorts our perception of life. Each of us perceives life from our backlog of experiences. Our memories are always with us, and they influence the way we perceive life, giving us a sense of expectancy. Our perceptions happen automatically, and we believe that what we perceive is the real world.

Therapist Richard F. Berg describes our ability to perceive as similar to a camera. Photographers can alter the image of reality through the use of various lenses or filters. Thus a camera might not provide an accurate view of the world. A telephoto lens has a narrower and more selective view of life; it can focus on a beautiful flower, but in so doing it shuts out the rest of the garden. Happy and smiling people seen through a fish-eye lens appear distorted and unreal. Filters can blur reality, break up images into pieces, bring darkness into a lighted scene, or even create a mist.

Like photographers' lenses and filters, depression distorts our perception of the world. Depression is like a set of camera filters which focus on the darker portions of life and take away the warmth, action, and joy from a scene. A photographer is aware of the distortion created by switching lenses. The depressed person, however, is not keenly aware of the distortion that he or she is creating as the lenses are switched. When we are depressed we are partially blind without knowing it. And the more intense our depression, the greater the distortion.[52]

What do we distort? We distort life itself. It loses its excitement and purpose. We distort the image of God. We see Him as far away and uncaring, separated from us by a tremendous gulf or wall. And we distort our own view of ourselves. Our value and abilities have vanished.

So far we have described some of the feelings and effects of depression. But what is it exactly? What have we learned over the years that might help us to define it better and understand what causes it?

Causes of Depression

In simple terms, depression is merely a negative emotion due to self-defeating perceptions and appraisals. However, it may also be a sign of serious, even malignant, disease. Depression is a term that can describe the "blahs" or the "blues," or it can describe a neurotic or psychotic disorder. Depression can be mild, moderate, or severe. It can be harmless or life-threatening.

Depression can be an inspiration to some creative people, but it can end in suicide for others. Depression can be a disorder, or merely a symptom of a disorder. For example, any of the symptoms of stress can be indicative of depression, and any of the symptoms of depression can be indicative of stress or some other specific ailment.

Depression can be found in babies less than one year old and in people who are more than 100 years old. In some individuals, depression may be readily observed by any layperson; in others it may be so masked that only experts can recognize it.

Depression can be caused by physical, mental, emotional, or spiritual problems, or by a combination of these. It can be caused by our self-defeating thinking or by separation from God. But it can also result from a shortage or malfunctioning of essential neurotransmitters in the brain.

Standard causes of depression include fatigue, insufficient or improper food, insufficient rest, reaction to medications, glandular imbalance, PMS, hypoglycemia, food allergies, low self-image, a pattern of negative thinking, behavior that contradicts your values, and postpartum issues.

Depression can result from major variables in atmospheric pressure, or perhaps lack of sunlight during the late fall and winter. A 31-year-old woman wrote, "I used to dread the fall.

When the leaves dropped, my mood would, too. I'd see the first leaves on the ground and I'd panic.... I couldn't work; I wouldn't want to wake up and I'd start putting on weight. I couldn't help it. Every fall I'd start this cycle that would last all winter. As soon as the days got longer and the green leaves started on the trees, I'd emerge again.... I often wished I was a bear so I could just go hibernate until spring. It seemed very sensible to me, and a lot less stressful than trying to maintain a regular life."[53]

Some joke about the weather affecting our moods. Well, for some people it is no joke. The words you just read describe a form of clinical depression known as *seasonal affective disorder* (SAD). This disorder is reflected by severe seasonal mood swings. These usually occur in late fall or early winter and last until spring, when the depression lifts. It appears to affect about four times as many men as women, especially those in their twenties and thirties. Those affected become listless and fatigued, sleep more, withdraw socially, feel anxious and irritable, and tend to gain weight. If these symptoms occur at least three different times and twice in consecutive years, then SAD is present.

The cause may be due to an underproduction of the hormone melatonin. Some researchers believe the reduced sunlight of winter affects the brain chemistry, since exposure to light lifts the depression. Those with SAD find relief by spending anywhere from 30 minutes to five hours a day in front of a special light box. This is not a tanning bed or just more lights. It's a special box containing several fluorescent tubes which give off the full amount of natural light at 10 to 20 times the intensity of indoor lighting.[54] For additional information about SAD see *Winter Blues,* by Norman E. Rosenthal, M.D.

One of the expressions of depression which is more and more in the limelight is what is referred to as "The Roller Coaster Illness." Bipolar or manic-depressive disorder involves wide-ranging mood cycles. A person's lows can be very low and his highs a mania, which gives the feeling there is nothing he cannot accomplish. The person has a euphoric or high feeling, becomes very active, and needs little sleep; his thoughts race, as well as being disconnected, and he feels the need to keep talking. Unimportant issues or events distract him, and he has inflated thoughts about his own capabilities. His behavior is impulsive and his judgment is poor. He can expect problems such as excessive spending, sexual acting out, and so on.

The person may be in this manic pattern for days and weeks, but then it all stops suddenly as he hits the other side of his mood swing. This is usually an inherited illness, and it continues to recur in the person's life. It is no respecter of gender, as it afflicts men and women in the same numbers. Various medications are used to treat this disease, with lithium as the most frequently prescribed. The "high" feeling or euphoria plus three or four other of the above symptoms need to exist in order for the symptoms to be classified as bipolar depression.

Is Depression a Sin?

One of the most common questions that Christians ask about depression concerns sin. "Is depression a sin? Is it a sin for a Christian to be depressed?" In and of itself depression is not sin. Depression is sometimes a *consequence* of sin, but not always. It can be a symptom of sin and thus serve as a warning to us. A husband who beats his wife or is unfaithful to her may experience both guilt and depression as a result of his behavior. He is being warned, and his depression is the consequence of what he is doing.

There has always been depression and there always will be. You're not alone in it. In fact, you're in good company. Many of the people who God used mightily in the Old Testament were so depressed they wanted to die—Moses, for example, plus Job, Elijah, Jonah, and certain writers of the Psalms (see especially Psalms 42 and 43). Great men and women throughout history have struggled with depression. So don't let anyone tell you that it's abnormal to be depressed, that it's a sin to be depressed, or that Christians don't experience depression. That is simply not true! Depression is a normal response to what is occurring in life.

Many people are surprised to read the account of Jesus' depression in the Garden of Gethsemane. Jesus was a perfect man and free from all sin, yet complete in His humanity and tempted as we are. Look at the account in Matthew 26:36-38:

> Then Jesus went with them to a place called Gethsemane, and He told His disciples, "Sit down here while I go over yonder and pray." And taking with Him Peter and the two sons of Zebedee, He began to show grief and distress of mind and was deeply depressed. Then He said to them, "My soul is very sad and deeply grieved, so that I am almost dying of sorrow. Stay here and keep awake and watch with Me" (AMP).

Jesus knew what was about to happen to Him, and it caused Him to be depressed. He did not feel guilty over being depressed, and neither should we. But this is sometimes difficult because our depression creates a distortion of life. It also intensifies any guilt feelings that we have. So guilt over depression leads to more depression.

Unfortunately, many of us have heard pastors preach that being depressed is a sin in and of itself. Every time I hear that, I cringe. I hurt for the people in the congregation who may be depressed. I wonder what that kind of message does to them.

Often when counseling a person experiencing depression I will ask, "Is there any way that you could thank God for being depressed?" The response is usually a puzzled look. Depression hurts. What could I possibly mean by thanking God for it? I might say, "Perhaps it is a signal that some other area of your life is crying out for recognition and help. If you weren't depressed you could be in even worse shape."

We need to see depression as a message to which we need to respond as soon as possible. As we look at the many causes for depression we will see why this is true. We will also note several people in the Scriptures who experienced depression, and we will explore what it meant in their lives.

What happens to us spiritually when depression occurs? Are there any predictable symptoms or tendencies? Two extremes occur. The most common is to withdraw from God. We tend not to pray or read the Scriptures as we once did. Why? Possibly because we feel that God has either rejected or abandoned us. Because guilt is a part of depression, we tend to feel that God is punishing us by rejecting us, and this creates our spiritual withdrawal. But God *does* understand what we are going through. He is neither rejecting nor punishing us. Cutting ourselves off from God only serves to reinforce our depression.

Just the opposite can also occur: A person may become overinvolved in spiritual things. This could be a compensation for the guilt that he feels. Hours are spent each day in prayer and reading the Scriptures, but it doesn't seem to lift the depression. This intense activity can actually limit the lifting of our depression, for we are neglecting other areas of our lives which need attention as well.

Three Stages of Depression

Perhaps you remember the story of the frog and the boiling water. If you drop a frog into a pan of cool water on the stove, it begins to swim about. It is enjoying itself. But if you turn on the flame under the pan and gradually warm up the water, the frog is not aware of the change in temperature. He is adjusting to the water as the temperature changes. In time the water becomes very hot, then boiling, and finally the frog is cooked. But the heat comes so gradually and subtly that the frog doesn't realize what is happening until it is too late.

Depression is like that: It is often difficult to detect in its early stages. We may experience some of the symptoms but not understand what they are until they intensify. And when we have moved deeper into depression, it is much more difficult to break its hold. Notice the three stages of depression described below.

THREE INTENSITIES
OF DEPRESSION

Light	Medium	Heavy
Low mood	These symptoms intensified	Very intensified
Minor loss of interest	Feelings of hopelessness	Either spiritual withdrawal or obsessive preoccupation
Thinking okay	Thinking painful and slow	
Knot in stomach	More preoccupied with self	
Eating and sleeping okay	Self-blame	*All of these symptoms could be intensified*
Slight spiritual withdrawal	Eating and sleeping a bit disturbed	

Light depression. Your mood may be a bit low or down. There is a slight loss of interest in what you normally enjoy. A few feelings of discouragement may also be present, but your thinking is still normal. There might be a few physical symptoms, but your sleeping and eating habits remain normal. There may be a slight spiritual withdrawal at times.

If you can recognize these symptoms as indications of depression (and if this is a reactionary depression), you are still in a position to reverse the depression. Ask yourself these questions: "What is my depression trying to tell me? What may be causing this reaction? What would be the best way to stabilize myself at this time? Would sharing this with another person help, and if so, who will I share this with? What

Scriptures would be helpful to read at this time, or what other resource would be helpful?" (Having a preplanned reading program in mind will be beneficial. This can include a devotional book and specific passages of Scripture. See the suggested passages at the conclusion of this book.) "What type of behaviors or activities would help me at this time?"

Medium depression. All of the previous symptoms will be intensified, but a prevailing feeling of hopelessness now emerges. Thinking is a bit slow as thoughts about yourself intensify. Tears may flow for no apparent reason. Sleeping and eating problems may emerge—either too much or too little. There is a greater struggle spiritually as the tendency to retreat from God increases. During this type of depression you will probably need the assistance of someone else to handle the depression. But your tendency may be to not share your difficulty with anyone else. This just intensifies your dilemma, however.

Severe depression. All of the previous symptoms occur and are very intense. Personal neglect is obvious. Appearance and cleanliness are ignored. Shaving or putting on makeup is neglected. It is a chore to complete daily tasks. Spiritual symptoms are obvious—either withdrawal or preoccupation. Crying is frequent, along with intense feelings of dejection, rejection, discouragement, self-blame, self-pity, and guilt. Patterns of eating and sleeping are disrupted.

A person who recognizes his light or mild depression does not want to have it, but often he does not know how to get rid of it. To keep from going into medium or deep depression, it is vital that we "let go" of our depression. Letting go before you plunge into the depths is the key to thwarting long-lasting and heavy depression. To illustrate this point, imagine that you are in a pool of deep water holding a heavy rock. The weight of the rock begins to pull you down. "I'm sinking," you say to yourself. What does that thought do to you? It makes you feel even worse. All you are aware of now is the fact that you are sinking. In time the surface of the water is over your head. You continue to sink lower and lower and you think, "I'm going down and down and down." This makes you feel worse, which makes you hold onto the rock even tighter and sink lower, and the vicious circle repeats itself.

Is the problem the fact that you are sinking? No! It is the rock. Let go of the rock, and then you'll have the opportunity to begin the journey back up to the surface.

Or perhaps you're swimming and you discover that you're a little more tired than you thought, or that the water is deeper and the current swifter than you expected. By taking action immediately you can quickly head for shore and avert a possible disaster. Hopefully you'll learn something from the experience. You can take similar action when you are in the light stage of depression.

But if the current is too strong, or if you're totally exhausted and on the verge of drowning, you will need the help of a lifeguard. If you are already in the medium or heavy stage of depression, or if your depression has immobilized you and you feel helpless, you need the help of someone who is loving, firm, empathetic, and a good listener to help pull you out.

Healthy and Unhealthy Depression

Depression is more easily understood when you can distinguish between healthy and unhealthy depression. A depression is healthy when you have *actual* feelings of pain, sadness, and disappointment (which may also include guilt, anger, and anxiety) from the negative experiences of life. This could include traumas, losses, discrimination, unfair treatment, and any unresolved hurt or damage. When depressed in this way you can still function, but not as well as you normally would.

Unhealthy depression, on the other hand, is an *inability to function* in any of the more basic areas of life—work, relationships, body functions, and so on—because of the depth of your bad feelings. It can arise from a multitude of factors including too many painfully unresolved experiences, genetic vulnerability, and changes in body chemistry.

One main distinction between healthy and unhealthy depression is the fact that healthy depressions are not usually biological in nature. Another main distinction is the degree to which the depressed person can function. Healthy depressions are less severe and can usually be resolved without professional help. Awareness and action are the key ingredients. You *can* face the world. But when you experience an unhealthy depression, you usually shut down as well as shut out the world.[55]

13

Depression in Women and Men

What about it? Are women more prone to depression than men? It appears so. At least two-thirds of those who are depressed are women, and some studies indicate that the ratio may be as high as six to one.[56] In 1990 the American Psychological Association convened a national Task Force on Women and Depression. Their findings showed that women were more depressed than men basically because of the challenges of being female in our contemporary culture.[57]

Some of the most recent findings on women's depression come from these studies and the work of Dr. Ellen McGraw, a clinical psychologist and specialist on women and depression.

What makes women more prone to depression than men? You may be surprised not only at the multitude of reasons but also at the wide variation. And some of the causes are more uniquely related to women than men.

Losses as a Source

Losses are often at the heart of many of the depressions of life, whether we're male or female. Any loss can trigger a reactive depression. It could be an actual or concrete loss involving something tangible: a person, a job, a home, a car, a valued photograph, a pet. The stronger the attachment, the more intense the feelings of loss. Especially devastating for

women—because they put so much of themselves into relationships and build strong attachments—is the loss of any
love relationship. Here is how Maggie Scarf describes this
dilemma, in her classic book *Unfinished Business:*

> It is around *losses of love* that the clouds of despair tend
> to converge, hover, and darken. Important figures leaving or
> dying; the inability to establish another meaningful bond with
> a peer-partner; being forced, by a natural transition in life, to
> relinquish an important love tie; a marriage that is ruptured,
> threatening to rupture, or simply growing progressively dis-
> tant; the splintering of a love affair or recognition that it is
> souring and will come to nothing. . . .[58]

Also potentially devastating are those losses that take
place only in your mind—the loss of love, hope, ambition,
self-respect, or other intangible elements of life. It could even
be a dream that disappears.

The most difficult type of loss to handle, however, is the
threatened loss. This loss has not yet occurred, but there is a
real possibility that it will happen. Waiting for the results of a
biopsy or a state bar exam, waiting to hear from the admis-
sions office of a college to which you have applied—situations
like this carry the possibility of loss. Depression can arise
because we feel powerless to do anything about the situation.
In a sense we are immobilized by threatened losses, overshad-
owed by depression. It is difficult to accept or deal with a loss
that hasn't yet occurred.

Life is full of threats. Some hang over our heads constantly and others come sweeping in with the force of a hur-
ricane. Some threatened losses can be handled by confronting
the threat and converting it into a real loss, if that is possible.
Others we must live with for a while. But living with the
threat of a loss is far easier if we share our pain with others.

Unfinished Business

Some of the depression experienced by women comes from the "unfinished business" that Maggie Scarf describes. It is possible to reach adulthood without being ready to be an adult. Some women have uncompleted growing tasks; they have never worked through the tasks of each stage of life. Perhaps they have never achieved a healthy separation from home. Or they may have left a psychological bill unpaid, such as an incestuous incident or relationship. They may be avoiding a pool of anger, such as a deeply held grudge.[59]

I have talked with many women who experience depression during the crucial transitions of life that take place during the twenties, thirties, or forties. For example, consider the woman in her thirties who is experiencing the turnarounds. During her twenties she made many choices, but during her thirties she wonders if she made the right ones. Perhaps it's best expressed in this way:

> The underlying theme of the turnarounds of the woman in her thirties is the crashing of the assumptions on which she had been living her life. She assumed she was making the right choices. She assumed she could always have children. She assumed she would always be young. That these are false assumptions becomes consciously real during the *thirties.*
>
> The woman who chose to stay home, who saw herself as a loving, nurturing mother, now wonders what she might have missed by not working. As her children enter school, she finds herself not being needed as she once was. She looks now at the working world as a place of fulfillment. If she has set aside goals in choosing to stay home, those goals surface again at this time, beckoning her to make a change.
>
> The woman who chose the nontraditional lane is experiencing a similar struggle. She looks at the full-time homemaker and wonders if she missed something. Maybe the

glamour of commuting to the office every day has worn off. Maybe she's tired of the rat race and being responsible for her share of the bills. Maybe the freedom she wanted so much now feels confining.

Maybe she put off that choice about having children. In her thirties, she sees time to have a family running out. The passing of age thirty signals to a woman that her prime time for reproduction physically has passed.[60]

And then in the middle years there are other losses. A woman can lose her mother role, identity, source, and physical attractiveness. She may grieve over not having become the person she might have been.[61]

Anger and Guilt

Both anger and guilt, mentioned earlier as companions of depression, can also cause depression. Unrecognized or unexpressed anger turns its fury inward looking for an object to punish; in this case it's yourself. Men tend to be more aggressive with their feelings, but if assertion is difficult for you, then you will tend to withdraw, feel powerless, seethe internally, and become depressed.

Guilt, too, is one of the standard causes of depression. Whether healthy or unhealthy, guilt that is left unresolved has to turn into something. That something is usually depression. And the depression left too long gains a foothold in your life.

Unrealistic expectations can also make us prone to depression; the higher our ideal is above the real, the greater our letdown will be. Unrealism can be an issue in beliefs about ourselves, others, or even our faith. Often it is a factor in relationships with men. And unmet expectations can lead to anger, which, if left undealt with, leads to . . . depression!

Inherited Depression

More and more research is being conducted on the question of whether depression or a predisposition toward depression can be inherited.

There is a point when any person would be over-whelmed by disaster. We all have our load limits. Painful experiences and emotional dilemmas appear in every person's life, but some seem to buckle under more easily than others. They appear to be predisposed to depression.[62]

Inherited depression has been defined as sad or bad feelings that occur when biological, genetic, cultural, or psychological depressions exist in a family and are passed down to the next generation as an increased vulnerability to both healthy and unhealthy depression. Sometimes this is disguised so well that it is hard to discern. The factors that are the most difficult to identify as depression are biological or genetic, or both. The symptoms may come out as addictions, eating disorders, or psychosomatic disorders. The tendency to depression can also be passed down by example, since people learn by example and observation. Relatives can pass down depressive ways of thinking and even behaving.[63]

Who in *your* family tree was depressed? Among the relatives, who were depressed? You might find it very helpful to think about and research this. You can begin by making a list of all your family-of-origin members; go back to your great-grandparents, and include aunts and uncles. You may have to interview family members or close family friends, but it will be worth the time and effort. As best you can, rate each of the family members you have listed on a scale of 1 to 10 for their level of depression. Use 1 for no depression or minimal depression, 2 to 5 for increasing degrees of healthy depression, and 6 to 10 for increasing degrees of unhealthy depression.[64]

While you're at it, ask yourself where *you* would fall on this scale currently . . . five years ago . . . as an adolescent . . . as a child. How much change, loss, stress, disappointment, physical illness, or trauma have you experienced in the past two years? In the last year? How have you responded to each situation? What type of support did you experience from others? Was there any anger associated with any of the events? If so, what did you do with it? Was it converted into depression?

How likely is it that depression will have an impact on your life? If you the reader are a woman, you have at least a one-in-four chance of experiencing a major unhealthy depression.[65] If your relatives, especially women, experienced severe neurotic depression or manic depression, you are two to three times more likely than other women to experience these depressions as well. In manic depression there seems to be a depression gene or genes, which could be inherited from either parent.[66]

If there are depression symptoms such as alcoholism or drug abuse among close relatives, you are eight to ten times more likely to develop similar symptoms. If a close relative committed suicide, you will be more vulnerable to suicide if you experience depression.[67]

What It Means for You

What does all this mean? *Don't ignore your depression.* Be aware. Look for alternatives to the way you are responding. See your depression as a message system telling you that something else is wrong. Look for the cause.

Healthy depression in women often has its roots in the interaction every person has with the world in which they live. If these challenges are met by taking constructive, coping steps which involve positive action as well as new ways of thinking, this can be a growth experience. If not, it can turn into an unhealthy depression. As you read on and discover the six types of healthy depression, reflect upon your life as it is now and as it has been. Perhaps these causes are at the core of what you are experiencing or have experienced in your life.

Victimization Depression

Many women experience *victimization depression*. These are the sad to bad feelings which develop from actual or learned helplessness, plus a lack of coping skills to handle the negativity, violence, and discrimination which women frequently face.

The feeling of being threatened can easily lead to a victim mentality. There are numerous ways in which women experience this. Some women are victimized emotionally when threatened by abandonment or violence. This might involve living in an environment of disrespect or devaluation. This is the most common form of emotional victimization for women; when it occurs early in life it can become a lifelong companion. Economic victimization occurs when a woman fails to receive equal or adequate pay for her work. Some women experience it when they're threatened economically if they don't conform to their parents' demands.

Being victimized physically is more than being beaten. It also includes being hurt through sexual contact. Bruises disappear, but the results of the trauma remain. Sexual victimization is one of the most traumatic of all; it involves anything from rape to phone calls to vague innuendos or threats.

Reflect upon your own life: Have you experienced any type of victimization? The first step is to identify it. Then look at the results, how you respond to it, and what you could do differently to break out of the pattern and thereby help lift your depression.[68]

Relationship Depression

A second type of depression is *relationship depression*. It too involves sad, mad, and bad feelings. But this depression is brought on either by the absence of a desired meaningful relationship or by the struggle, conflict, disappointment, hurts, and mistrust that can be experienced in maintaining a relationship. Relationship depression can occur because of a low self-image which hinders us from having the desired relationship, or because of a lack of the relational skills needed to have a relationship. Women are especially vulnerable in this area.

Why is this? Perhaps one reason is that women are taught early in life to be more vulnerable to relationship depression. They usually assume too much responsibility for keeping a relationship going; if it fails they tend to blame themselves. Relationship problems are thus seen as personal failures. Another reason for this depression is that too many women deny the fact that relationships can be very painful. They suffer in silence, not sharing their fears, protests, desires, wants, and hurts. Perhaps it would help to identify in advance what one wants in a relationship and then move more slowly into it in order to evaluate the other person's potential.

Age Rage Depression

If you don't identify with the next type of depressive response now, you probably will someday. It's called *age rage depression*. This is the healthy reaction of bad feelings that a woman experiences because of aging in a society that idolizes youth and sees female aging as representing a series of irreplaceable losses. Aging, we have been taught, is a time of life in which there is less of everything that is of value; it means growing less attractive and less able to function physically in numerous ways. Aging is dreaded by women in our society. Men often gain respect as they grow older, but women are devalued by our culture.

Three of the contributors to this problem are the healthcare system, the cosmetics industry, and (as you probably know) the media. Women are constantly bombarded by messages that they must be young or at least try to look and dress young—and they respond by pressuring themselves to the extreme. When women are given recommendations about health care, this advice is usually based on knowledge about men's diseases and needs rather than research on women's health. We hear much about men and heart attacks, yet very little about this as a major cause of death for women.

Aging is not a condition that you can prevent; we're all growing older. But while you can't change your aging losses, you can change how you view them and respond to them. Aging doesn't have to be seen as a loss of opportunities and independence. But to fight age rage depression, you must take charge of how you view yourself. Though others may be bemoaning their age and apologizing for it, you must learn to react counter to our culture. Try making an "Age Gains" list and identify the positives of growing older. Any such antici-patory planning can move you from being a victim to being a woman of confidence.[69]

Body-Image Depression

A related source of depression is when you buy into soci-ety's myth that equates your value with your appearance. Known as *body-image depression*, this causes many women to struggle with feelings of shame, contempt, or disappointment about their bodies. It stems from the struggle to meet cultural standards of beauty, physical perfection, and sex appeal, which are unrealistic and unattainable.[70]

Depletion Depression

Most women I know have experienced some form of *depletion depression*. This comes from being overwhelmed, exhausted, stressed, and just basically drained because of role demands and conflicts. Trying to juggle everything can lead to the feeling of running on empty, as well as to despair. Your feelings are an appropriate response to all the demands you face, whether your lifestyle is traditional or nontraditional. Feelings of fatigue and depletion are probably more extreme today than ever before because of the current economic and emotional battles that women must engage in. You can't do it all, regardless of your expectations and those of others. Working mothers, whether married or single, feel the drain especially; there just isn't sufficient time or energy for every-thing. As fatigue is one of the major causes for anger, so it is for depression.

Some women have found that it works wonders to make a list of everything (and I mean *everything*) they do during the day. They study the list, gradually eliminating some items and turning that time into sleep! The books *How to Get Control of*

Your Time and Your Life, by Alan Lakein, and *When I Relax I feel Guilty*, by Tim Hansel, may be helpful.

Mind-Body Depression

Mind-body depression is no stranger to women, and there are three varieties. Your body can create the depression in your mind, or the depression can occur because of the physical problems your mind creates for your body. Mind-body depression can also be expressed as physical symptoms rather than feelings. The last form is purely the result of hormonal and biochemical changes which occur in women at different phases in their life. These include menstruation, pregnancy, postpartum fluctuations, menopause, postmenopause, or any assortment of biochemical imbalances. Research indicates that anywhere from 20 to 80 percent of women experience some form of PMS, which is often closely linked to depression. Two of the most helpful resources for some of these issues are *Premenstrual Syndrome* by Niels H. Lauersen, M.D., and *Menopause and Mid-life*, by Robert G. Wells, M.D., and Mary C. Wells.

Male Depression

Men also experience depression. Many more men than we ever realize experience this condition. Many of them conceal this struggle from the outside world. Not only do they camouflage it carefully from others, but all too often from themselves as well. We call what many men experience *covert* rather than *overt* depression. But it can still drive what a man does. This masked depression can drive a man to work more to numb the pain. Or he may display it by anger. Some men try to drown their discontent with alcohol.[71]

When depression is masked, a man is not only cut off from the reality of his condition but also from any possibility of comfort from others. Culture must bear a portion of the culprits responsible for the epidemic of covert depression in our society. Traditional masculinity views not only the strong expressions of emotion as unmanly, but also prohibits most expressions of vulnerability. A man should always "be strong."

Room for anything else is not available. Many men experience shame if they reveal their vulnerability, so depression is not admitted or talked about. A depressed man finds that the condition itself is unacceptable to his male image.

Culture also helps to perpetuate the myth that men shouldn't reach out for help but be self-reliant. So the wounds that foster depression aren't shared.[72]

The silence of a man is designed to protect him against the fact that he does have needs and against needing other people. Unfortunately, the silence is a lie that damages and weakens a man even more.

Many men have been wounded or traumatized as children, and they learn to freeze their feelings. Depression is a freezing process. When a man is able to allow his covert depression to become overt it may be experienced as grief, which is good. Grief is a cure for depression. The loss of being wounded needs recognition and release. When a man quits trying to numb his feelings they can be expressed. And then he can discover that his fear that expression or crying once begun will never stop is actually unfounded.

14

*O*vercoming
Depression

Complex and confusing—that's how people react to this malady we call depression. But keep in mind that it has a purpose: to alert you to whatever is causing the problem so you can eliminate the cause.

The initial step is to admit that what you are experiencing is depression. Put a name to it and don't ignore what is taking place in your life.

It is important to confront and work through your depression, and there are four good reasons.

1. *Later regrets.* If you fail to let go of depression you take a chance of doing something that you will regret later, when the depression lifts. Depressed persons sometimes make disastrous mistakes while they are depressed. They have gone so far as to quit their jobs or walk out on their marriages. When the depression lifts, they look back and think, "How could I have ever done such a thing?"

2. *Compounded problems.* If you fail to let go of a depression, you set yourself up for more hurt. This is called the "depressive theorem." Feeling bad seems to bring about situations in which bad things happen. These events then serve to deepen our depression, confirming the many bad things we suspected about ourselves. These compounded

problems can be traced to a depressed person's weakened ability to cope and flex.

3. *Chronic depression.* If you fail to let go of a depression you set yourself up for chronic or habitual depression. Depression becomes your primary way of responding to life's disappointments.

4. *Possible self-destruction.* If you fail to let go of a depression you set yourself up for suicidal tendencies. If the depression lingers unchecked, it can lead to hopelessness, making life nothing but a horrible nightmare. All a depressed person can remember are moments of suffering; the good moments are blotted out.[73]

If you find you are becoming depressed, what can you do about it? First of all, check for any physical reasons for your depression. You may want to see your medical doctor for this. If there is no physical cause, then your next step is to ask yourself two key questions. You may even want to ask your mate or a good friend to help you think them through.

1. Is my depression in any way related to the six healthy depressions previously discussed? If so, what does that tell me I need to do at this time in my life?

2. Am I doing anything that might be contributing to my depression? Check your behavior to determine that it is consistent with Scripture and your values. Ask yourself if you are doing anything to reinforce the depression.

What to Do About Depression

Look for your depression "trigger." Some triggers are obvious: You're readily aware of what prompted the depression. Other causes are more difficult to discover. To help you track them down, you may want to write the following questions on a card: What did I do? Where did I go? With whom did I speak? What did I see? What did I read? What was I thinking?

Refer to this card when you're depressed; it may help if you recall the thought or event that triggered the depression.

Please do not attempt to deal with your depression by yourself. Reading the recommended books for this section may help you, but if the depression has been with you for some time, talk to a trusted friend and seek out a professional Christian counselor. But do something. The lethargy that is a by-product of being depressed causes us to behave in a way that reinforces our depression. Let me suggest what Brenda Poinsett recommends; she experienced a deep depression herself and writes about it in her book *Why Do I Feel This Way?* If you are experiencing any of the symptoms she mentions below, please seek out someone trained in helping others with their depression. These suggestions are applicable to men as well.

We need help when we don't know what caused the depression. The black cloud of despair came out of nowhere. The despair is dark and deep, and in all honesty we cannot fathom a cause.

We need help if we are having suicidal thoughts.

We need help if we are having delusional thoughts.

We need help if we can't sleep, or we are losing a serious amount of weight, or we are experiencing severe physical discomfort in which our health may be affected.

We need help if we have had repeated depressive episodes in our life.

We need help when the depression is hurting our marriage, our family, or our job.

We definitely need help if the depression has lasted longer than one year.

A person fitting any of these conditions needs to consider seeking outside help in getting over her depression. Depression is a treatable illness. While there is not one simple cure that works for everyone, there are a number of treatments available.[74]

If one method doesn't bring you out of depression, another likely will. Anyone suffering from depression needs to know how to get help and what kind is available.

When Do You Need Counseling?

There are times when a person will benefit the most in his or her struggle with depression by counseling or medication or both. If you experience depressive episodes frequently (daily to several times a week), with the symptoms lasting for a two-week period or longer and with intensity, you may want to seek counseling. The depressive tendency to isolate yourself may inhibit you from taking the necessary steps to get help. Don't keep your depression to yourself. Let others who are knowledgeable and caring know what your struggles are and let them help you.

In many cases medication has helped to break the incessant cycle of being depressed. Medication is nothing to be afraid of or avoided. I have seen it help many people. There are many different types of medication available today, including Prozac, Zoloft, Paxil, Nardil, Parnate, Enovil, and many others. These are to be prescribed and used only under the care of a physician or a psychiatrist. Some have definite side effects, and it is not uncommon for one medication to be changed to another or the dosage adjusted in order to find the right combination. (See Chapter 15 of Brenda Poinsett's book *Why Do I Feel Depressed?* or Chapter 9 of Robert Hirschfield's *When the Blues Won't Go Away* for additional information on medication.)

Another thing you can do if you find yourself becoming depressed is to evaluate your thoughts and value judgments. This is very important, because if your thinking pattern is negative and you persist in making negative value judgments about yourself, depression will result.

First, recognize and identify the thoughts that you express to yourself. When something happens and you experience depression, you need to realize that there is more than the outward event behind your feelings. Perhaps you had a negative thought or made a negative value judgment regarding the thing that happened. This sets you up for depression.

Second, realize that many of your thoughts are automatic. They are involuntary. You don't have to think about having them—they just pop in. They are not the result of deliberation or reasoning. But if you reason against them you can put them aside.

Third, distinguish between ideas and facts. Just because you may think something does not mean it is true. If you are depressed because you feel that your spouse doesn't like the way you dress or the meals you cook, check with him. You may be right—but you could also be wrong. If you make an assumption, always try to see if it is true.

Finally, whenever you discover that a particular thought is not true, state precisely why it is inaccurate or invalid. This step is vital! Putting the reasons into words helps you in three ways: It actually reduces the number of times the idea will recur, it decreases the intensity of the idea, and it tones down the feeling or mood that the idea generates. The more you counteract your negative ideas in this way, the more your depression is lessened.

Positive Steps to Take

Begin your positive steps in overcoming depression by asking yourself these three questions:

1. What is my depression doing for me? Am I getting anything out of being depressed?

2. Have I undergone any major changes or stresses during the past few months or years? What are they? How am I trying to adjust to them?

3. What kind of environment am I in? Is it helping me to come out of my depression, or could it be making me more depressed?

Then undertake the following additional steps.

1. Look at your eating and sleeping habits to see if they ought to be changed.

2. Are you following your normal routine of life or are you withdrawing by staying in bed longer, staying away from friends, letting the dishes stack up in the sink, and avoiding regular activities? Are you cutting yourself off from your friends and family? If so, it is important to force yourself to stay active, as hard as it might seem. Remember that a depressed person begins behaving and acting in such a way that the depression is reinforced. You must break the depressive pattern of behavior by yourself or by asking someone to help you.

3. If you're married, let your spouse know that you are depressed. Ask him or her to listen as you explain it. If you want him to comment, let him do so; but if not, tell him you would rather he didn't. If you are angry with him, or with anyone, discuss your feelings with the person and get them out into the open.

4. Each day, either by yourself or with another person's help, make a list of what you would do during the day if you were not depressed. After you have made this list in detail, work out a plan to follow what is on that list each day.

Another way of developing a pattern of positive behavior is to make an extensive list (with help if necessary) of pleasant events. After the list is made, select several events to do each day. This "pleasant events" schedule is not a panacea for all depression, but often you can break the pattern of depression through your behavior. Most people feel better when they engage in pleasant activities.

Focusing and dwelling upon positive Scriptures will also help you. Each morning read these passages; put them on posters and place them around the house: Psalm 27:1-3; 37:1-7; Isaiah 26:3; 40:28-31.

Is it possible to pray one's way out of depression? Some people have tried to do so but have found no change. It depends upon the type or cause of depression. If sin is the direct cause of depression, then prayer which includes confession, repentance, and the acceptance of forgiveness can rid you of the depression. But all too often the depressed individual *thinks* his depression is caused by sin when in reality it is not. This is often a reflection of the person's feeling of worthlessness, which accompanies depression.

Some people advocate praising God as a means of defeating depression. Genuine praise for who God is and for the strength that He gives us can be an aid in handling our depression. However, waiting until we feel like praising Him will hamper us, for in a depressed state we probably do not feel full of praise. Taking the time and energy to sit and list our blessings and then specifically mentioning them to God in prayer may give us a better perspective. The best way of doing this is with another person who is not depressed and knows your life quite well.

Becoming More Active

When you are experiencing depression, one of the best remedies is to become more active. Changing one's level of activity has several benefits, but it is often difficult to do. It means going counter to what you are feeling. The first step in increasing your activity is to discover the good reasons which are strong enough to make you try. Second, you need to challenge the thoughts and ideas which you are using or will use to keep you from being active.

Increasing your activity is a definite way of changing your thinking. When you do less, you think of yourself as inadequate, lazy, and worthless. A good reason to become more active is to challenge those ideas; by being more active you create evidence that you are not like that. You show yourself that you can get started and accomplish something.

Studies indicate that activity will improve your mood. Usually the more you do, the better you feel. It also provides a helpful diversion from your depression by distracting your mind from unpleasant thoughts.

Activity will also counteract the fatigue which you find with depression. It is a paradox with depression that when you are depressed, you need to do more to gain more energy. When you are not depressed, you are revived by rest and inactivity. Studies also show that activity will increase our motivation. By completing a simple task successfully, you will be motivated to try some other task. With depression there is another seeming paradox: You must do what you don't feel like doing before you will feel like doing it! This is strange, but true. And this phenomenon is not limited to a depressed state, for many people find that by doing a behavior first, their feelings come in line with that behavior.

By being active you can stimulate yourself to think. Thus your mental ability is stimulated as well. New solutions to previously unsolvable situations are discovered.

When you become more active you find that other people positively reinforce what you are doing. You no longer have to hear them suggest that you "do something."

The following is an activity record to help keep track of your activities. This written exercise is important because when you are depressed you do not remember the positive as well as the negative. Selective remembering is in progress. Be aware of what you write. You may tend to write down a negative, such as "I just did nothing." But perhaps your doing nothing involved watching a TV program and drinking a cup of tea. Record that activity instead, since that is doing something. Record hour by hour what you do for a week. Next to the actual activity indicate how much satisfaction you felt on a scale from 0 to 5 (0 meaning none and 5 meaning great).

This tabulation can help you see what it is that gives you pleasure and satisfaction.

WEEKLY ACTIVITY SCHEDULE

	S	M	T	W	Th	F	S
9–10							
10–11							
11–12							
12–1							
1–2							
2–3							
3–4							
4–5							
5–6							
6–7							
7–8							
8–12							

It is also important for you to plan an actual schedule of what you will do. By scheduling your activities you are once more taking control of your life. It will also help you overcome indecisiveness, which is a common characteristic of depression. Keeping a schedule and scheduling activities will give you an opportunity to identify and counter the self-defeating thoughts which keep you immobilized. By reviewing what you have already done and by looking over what you plan to do the next day, you will begin to have a different set of feelings about yourself.

If you miss an activity, just let it go and schedule it another time. If you finish a task early, don't start the next task until the set time. Do something enjoyable until that time. Schedule activities in half-hour and one-hour intervals, and don't plan activities that are too specific or too general. Don't bite off more than you can chew. Enjoying the activity at a satisfying pace is part of the plan.

If you have let the house go for several weeks, it may take several weeks or days to establish some order. That extended time is all right! Break your tasks down into smaller ones. Grade them from easy to difficult. List the various jobs which need to be done, whether your task is to clean the basement, the yard, or the living room. List what you will do within that overall job. Cleaning the living room may involve picking up all the magazines, dusting, vacuuming, washing the two windows, getting the dog hair off the easy chair, and so forth.

Don't be surprised if you are tempted to skip scheduling your activities. Here are some typical sabotage techniques you may try to use on yourself and some ways to counter them.

Statement: "I don't know if I can think of any activities to schedule."

Answer: You are probably having trouble thinking of any. Why not list activities that you must do each day (such as eating and dressing), activities that give you pleasure, and activities that bring a sense of accomplishment?

Statement: "I have never kept records and I have never been able to work under a schedule."

Answer: Scheduling is a simple skill which can be learned. If it is difficult for you to keep an hour-by-hour schedule, you could list one task from 8:00–10:00, another from 10:00–12:00, and one from 1:00–6:00. This is a good way to begin.

Statement: "I have so much difficulty with distractions. I just do not follow through."

Answer: Make a list of the typical distractions. Identify what they are, and then in writing formulate how you will refuse to give in to each distraction. You may need to unplug the TV, phone, and home computer and reconnect them when the task is completed. It is also all right to tell a caller that you are busy but will talk to him or her at a later time.

Write yourself a contract, such as "I will complete 30 minutes of housecleaning and then read *Redbook* for 20 minutes."

Use signs around the house to remind you of your commitments and schedule. Make them odd and different in order to attract your attention. When you start a task, select the easiest and simplest one so that you are almost guaranteed success.

15

A Better Life

Can you imagine your life being better after your depression than before? Unlikely though it may seem, many people have experienced exactly this phenomenon. Remember the passage in the last chapter of Job (42:12). Through your depression, you can develop a new perspective about life, a greater awareness of your identity and your abilities, a new way of seeing and relating to others, and a deeper relationship with God. This latter step occurs as you feed on His Word, especially on verses like these:

> Keep me safe, O God, for in you I take refuge (Psalm 16:1).
>
> I have set the LORD always before me. Because he is at my right hand, I will not be shaken (Psalm 16:8).
>
> You, O LORD, keep my lamp burning; my God turns my darkness into light (Psalm 18:28).
>
> The LORD is my light and my salvation—whom shall I fear? The Lord is the stronghold of my life—of whom shall I be afraid? (Psalm 27:1).
>
> Hear my voice when I call, O LORD; be merciful to me and answer me (Psalm 27:7).
>
> God is our refuge and strength, an ever-present help in trouble (Psalm 46:1).
>
> Have mercy on me, O God, according to your unfailing love; according to your great compassion blot out my transgressions (Psalm 51:1).

How do you feel about yourself as a person? How do you view yourself? Is it the same as how God sees you? Reflecting on God's Word will reveal the truth about who you are and who God is, and this is the basis for changing your perception of who you are.

Our understanding of who God is and how He wants to work in our lives is enriched when we realize that He is committed to performing good in our lives. Consider what God's Word says about this: "Surely goodness and love will follow me all the days of my life, and I will dwell in the house of the LORD forever" (Psalm 23:6). "I will make an everlasting covenant with them: I will never stop doing good to them. . . . I will rejoice in doing them good and will assuredly plant them in this land with all my heart and soul" (Jeremiah 32:40,41).

A few years ago the choir at our church sang an anthem based on Zephaniah 3:14,17. I had never heard this song before. The words were printed in our church bulletin, and I have read them many times since then because they encourage me, inspire me, and remind me of what I mean to God:

> And the Father will dance over you in joy!
> He will take delight in whom He loves.
> Is that a choir I hear singing the praises of God?
> No, the Lord God Himself is exulting over you in song!
> And He will joy over you in song!
> My soul will make its boast in God,
> For He has answered all my cries.
> His faithfulness to me is as sure as the dawn of a new day.
> Awake, my soul, and sing!
> Let my spirit rejoice in God!
> Sing, O daughter of Zion, with all of your heart!
> Cast away fear, for you have been restored!
> Put on the garment of praise as on a festival day.
> Join with the Father in glorious, jubilant song.
> God rejoices over you in song![75]

Does that say something to you about your value in the sight of God? Does that fling open the doors of possibility for you to make choices in your life that will lead to hope and eventually to freedom from depression?

Another help, I've found, is to read this paraphrase of 1 Corinthians 13:4-8 each day. Do this each day for a month, along with everything else you are doing to counter your depression, and it will gently and gradually change your perception of yourself.

Because God loves me he is slow to lose patience with me.

Because God loves me he takes the circumstances of my life and uses them in a constructive way for my growth.

Because God loves me he has no need to impress me with how great and powerful he is because *he is God,* nor does he belittle me as his child in order to show me how important he is.

Because God loves me he is for me. He wants to see me mature and develop in his love.

Because God loves me he does not send down his wrath on every little mistake I make, of which there are many.

Because God loves me he does not keep score of all my sins and then beat me over the head with them whenever he gets the chance.

Because God loves me he is deeply grieved when I do not walk in the ways that please him, because he sees this as evidence that I don't trust him and love him as I should.

Because he loves me he rejoices when I experience his power and strength and stand up under the pressures of life for his Name's sake.

Because God loves me he keeps on working patiently with me even when I feel like giving up and can't see why he doesn't give up with me, too.

Because God loves me he never says there is no hope for me; rather, he patiently works with me, loves me and disciplines me in such a way that it is hard for me to understand the depth of his concern for me.

Because God loves me he never forsakes me, even though many of my friends might.

Because God loves me he stands with me when I have reached the rock bottom of despair, when I see the real me and compare that with his righteousness, holiness, beauty, and love. It is at a moment like this that I can really believe that God loves me.

Yes, the greatest gift of all is God's perfect love![76]

RECOMMENDED READING ON DEPRESSION

Hart, Archibald D. *Dark Clouds, Silver Lining.* Colorado Springs: Focus on the Family, 1993.

Hirschfield, Robert, M.D. *When the Blues Won't Go Away: New Approaches to Dysthmic Disorder and Other Forms of Chronic Low-Grade Depression.* New York: MacMillan, 1991.

McGraw, Ellen. *When Feeling Bad Is Good: An Innovative Self-Help Program for Women to Convert Healthy Depression into New Sources of Growth and Power.* New York: Henry Holt, 1992.

Notes

1. James R. Beck and David T. Moore, *Helping Worriers* (Grand Rapids: Baker Books, 1994), p. 26.

2. Original source unknown.

3. John Haggai, *How to Win Over Worry* (Eugene, OR: Harvest House Publishers, 1987), pp. 16-17.

4. Edward M. Hallowell, *Worry* (New York: Pantheon Books, 1997), p. 73, adapted.

5. Ibid., p. 9, adapted.

6. Beck and Moore, *Helping*, pp. 31-33, adapted.

7. Hallowell, *Worry*, p. 5, adapted.

8. O. Quentin Hyder, *The Christian's Handbook of Psychiatry* (Old Tappan, NJ: Fleming H. Revell, 1971).

9. Earl Lee, *Recycle for Living* (Ventura, CA: Regal Books, 1973), p. 4.

10. Samuel H. Kraines and Eloise S. Thetford, *Help for the Depressed* (Springfield, IL: Charles C. Thomas, 1979), pp. 190-91.

11. Hallowell, *Worry*, p. 67.

12. Ibid., pp. 56-65, adapted.

13. Lucinda Bassett, *From Panic to Power* (New York: Harper Collins, 1995), pp. 32-33, adapted.

14. Ibid., pp. 70-80, adapted.

15. Ibid., pp. 156-157, adapted.

16. Beck and Moore, *Helping*, pp. 19-20, adapted.

17. Hallowell, *Worry*, p. 39, adapted.

18. Elizabeth Skoglund, *To Anger with Love* (New York: Harper & Row, 1977), p. 32.

19. Dennis and Matthew Linn, *Healing Life's Hurts* (New York: Paulist Press, 1978), pp. 102-03, adapted.

20. For a discussion of these and other related studies see Matthew McKay, Peter D. Rogers, and Judith McKay, *When Anger Hurts* (Oakland, CA: New Harbinger Publications, 1989), pp. 23-32, adapted; and Redford Williams, *The Trusting Heart* (New York Time: 1989), pp. 49-71, adapted.

21. Joseph Cooke, *Celebration of Grace* (Grand Rapids: Zondervan, 1991) N.P. Previously published as *Free for the Taking* (Revell, 1975), pp. 109-110.

22. Elizabeth Skoglund, *Anger*, pp. 78-79, adapted.

23. Gary Hawkins with Carol Hawkins, *Prescription for Anger* (New York: Warner Books, 1988), pp. 45-51, adapted.

24. See footnote 3 on page 125 of *How to Frustration-Proof Your Communication*.

25. Hawkins and Hawkins, *Prescription*, pp. 196-98, adapted.

26. H. Norman Wright, *So You're Getting Married* (Ventura, CA: Regal Books, 1987), p. 130.

27. Aaron T. Beck, *Love Is Never Enough* (New York: Harper & Row, 1988); idea adapted from pp. 270-74 and communication experiments over several years of counseling with couples.

28. Ibid., pp. 274-76, adapted.

29. David Viscott, *I Love You, Let's Work It Out* (New York: Simon & Schuster, 1987) pp. 177-78, adapted.

30. Mark P. Cosgrove, *Counseling for Anger* (Dallas: Word, 1988), p. 120, adapted.

31. Lewis Smedes, *Forgive and Forget* (New York: Harper & Row, 1989), p. 37.

32. H. Norman Wright, *Making Peace with Your Past* (Grand Rapids: Baker/Revell, 1985), pp. 66-69, adapted.

33. Richard P. Walters, *Anger, Yours and Mine and What to Do About It* (Grand Rapids: Zondervan Publishing House, 1981), pp. 150-51.

34. Judson Edwards, *Regaining Control of Your Life* (Minneapolis: Bethany House Publishers, 1989), pp. 15-16.

35. Georgia Witkin-Lanoil, *The Female Stress Syndrome: How to Recognize and Live With It*, 2nd ed. (New York: New Market, 1991), pp. 16-17, adapted.

36. Sheila West, *Beyond Chaos: Stress Relief for the Working Woman* (Colorado Springs: NavPress, 1992), p. 104, adapted.

37. Ibid., pp. 106-07.

38. Witkin-Lanoil, *Female Stress*, pp. 118-19, adapted.

39. Ibid., pp. 125-26.

40. Ibid., pp. 118-21.

41. American Psychological Association National Task Force on Women and Depression, "Women and Depression: Risk Factor and Treatment Issues" (Washington D.C.: The American Psychological Association, 1990); as cited in Witkin-Lanoil, *Female Stress*, p. 122.

42. *Keri Report*, "The State of American Women Today" (Bristol-Meyer, 1991).

43. L. Dotto, *Losing Sleep* (New York: William-Morrow, 1990).

44. Adapted from A.T. Oafexis, "Drowsy America," in *Time*, December 1990, p. 78.

45. Ellen McGraw, *When Feeling Bad Is Good* (New York: Henry Holt & Co, 1992), p. 206, adapted.

46. Adapted from *Keri Report*, pp. 132-33.

47. Ibid., p. 91.

48. Ibid., p. 102.

49. Gary J. Oliver and H. Norman Wright, *Good Women Get Angry* (Ann Arbor, MI: Servant Publications, 1995), pp. 124-31, adapted.

50. Lloyd John Ogilvie, *God's Best for My Life* (Eugene, OR: Harvest House, 1981), February 3.

51. Suggestions adapted from Archibald Hart, *Preventing Burnout and Stress* (Fuller Seminary Alumni Report, March 1984) p. 20.

52. Richard F. Berg, C.S.C. and Christine McCartney, *Depression and the Integrated Life* (New York: Alba House, 1981), pp. 34, 35, adapted.

53. Julia Thorne with Larry Rothstein, *You Are Not Alone* (New York: Harper Collins, 1992), p. 129.

54. Brenda Poinsett, *Why Do I Feel This Way?* (Colorado Springs: NavPress, 1996), pp. 36, 37, adapted.

55. McGraw, *Feeling Bad*, pp. 22-25, adapted.

56. Poinsett, *Feel*, p. 17, adapted.

57. McGraw, *Feeling Bad*, p. 17, adapted.

58. Maggie Scarf, *Unfinished Business: Pressure Points in the Lives of Women* (New York: Doubleday, 1985), pp. 86-87.

59. Poinsett, *Feel*, pp. 98, 99, adapted.

60. Ibid., pp. 82-83.

61. Ibid., pp. 86-87, adapted.

62. Ibid., p. 44.

63. McGraw, *Feeling Bad*, pp. 34-39, adapted.

64. Ibid., p. 46.

65. Ellen McGraw, et al., *Women and Depression: Risk Factor and Treatment Issues* (Washington D.C.: American Psychological Association, 1990), p. 2, adapted.

66. D.F. Papolos and J. Papolos, *Overcoming Depression* (New York: Harper & Row, 1988), p. 47, adapted.

67. M. Goed, *The Good News About Depression* (New York: Bantam, 1986), pp. 195-203, adapted.

68. McGraw, *Feeling Bad*, pp. 75-86, adapted.

69. Ibid., pp. 154-78, adapted.

70. Ibid., p. 223, adapted.

71. Terrence Real, *I Don't Want to Talk About It* (New York: Scribner, 1997), pp. 40-41, adapted.

72. Ibid., p. 148, adapted.

73. Poinsett, *Feel*, pp. 115-17, adapted.

74. Ibid., pp. 131-32.

75. "And the Father Will Dance." Lyrics adapted from Zephaniah 3:14,17 and Psalm 54:2,4. Arranged by Mark Hayes.

76. Dick Dickinson, INTERFACE *Psychological Services* (Fullerton, CA).

Other Books
By H. Norman Wright

AFTER YOU SAY I DO
by *H. Norman Wright and Wes and Judy Roberts*

Couples will find a wealth of practical ideas for enriching their future together. Includes: how to resolve conflict in marriage, setting goals, handling finances, and building healthy in-law relationships.

BEFORE YOU SAY I DO
by *H. Norman Wright*

With over 500,000 copies sold, this guide is now revised and updated for the 90's. Couples will explore how to clarify role expectations, establish a healthy sexual relationship, handle finances, and acquire a solid understanding of how to develop a biblical relationship.

QUIET TIMES FOR COUPLES
by *H. Norman Wright*

Designed to stimulate genuinely open communication between husband and wife, each day's devotion makes it easy for couples to share about the deeper parts of their lives.

TRAINING CHRISTIANS TO COUNSEL
by *H. Norman Wright*

A first-of-a-kind manual for training mature laymen to effectively counsel others in their church, community, or crisis center in areas such as divorce, remarriage, bereavement, suicide, and depression.

Dear Reader,

We would appreciate hearing from you regarding this Harvest House nonfiction book. It will enable us to continue to give you the best in Christian publishing.

1. What most influenced you to purchase *Winning over Your Emotions?*
   - ❑ Author
   - ❑ Subject matter
   - ❑ Backcover copy
   - ❑ Recommendations
   - ❑ Cover/Title
   - ❑ Other_____

2. Where did you purchase this book?
   - ❑ Christian bookstore
   - ❑ General bookstore
   - ❑ Department store
   - ❑ Grocery store
   - ❑ Other_____

3. Your overall rating of this book?
   ❑ Excellent ❑ Very good ❑ Good ❑ Fair ❑ Poor

4. How likely would you be to purchase other books by this author?
   ❑ Very likely ❑ Not very likely ❑ Somewhat likely ❑ Not at all

5. What types of books most interest you? (Check all that apply.)
   - ❑ Women's Books
   - ❑ Marriage Books
   - ❑ Current Issues
   - ❑ Christian Living
   - ❑ Bible Studies
   - ❑ Fiction
   - ❑ Biographies
   - ❑ Children's Books
   - ❑ Youth Books
   - ❑ Other_____

6. Please check the box next to your age group.
   ❑ Under 18 ❑ 18-24 ❑ 25-34 ❑ 35-44 ❑ 45-54 ❑ 55 and over

Mail to: Editorial Director
Harvest House Publishers
1075 Arrowsmith
Eugene, OR 97402

Name _____

Address _____

State _____ Zip _____

Thank you for helping us to help you in future publications!

100699